THE
NEW
BIRTH

by

EVANGELIST OLIVER B. GREENE

THE GOSPEL HOUR, INC.
Oliver B. Greene, Founder
Box 2024, Greenville, S. C. 29602

First printing, September 1966 — 10,000 copies
Second printing, November 1967 — 10,000 copies
Third printing, January 1969 — 15,000 copies
Fourth printing, July 1970 — 15,000 copies
Fifth printing, June 1973 — 15,000 copies
Sixth printing, November 1974 — 15,000 copies
Seventh printing, April 1980 — 10,000 copies

FOREWORD

The messages in this book are sermons the Lord has used to the salvation of lost souls and the uplifting of God's people in our evangelistic meetings. I trust they will be used to reach many other souls as they go out in this volume. Not all people find it possible to attend church services; not all have the opportunity to listen to radio messages—but almost everyone can find a few minutes each day to read. The Gospel is "the power of God unto salvation to every one that believeth"—and my prayer is that many will believe and be saved through reading these messages.

The Author

CONTENTS

The New Birth

THE NEW BIRTH

CHAPTER I

"Except a Man Be Born Again"

Did our Lord Jesus Christ come into the world to make men moral, or did He come into the world to do more than make us moral? In this message we shall answer that question according to the Word of God.

Peter speaks to us in these inspired words: "For Christ also hath once suffered for sins, the just for the unjust, that He might bring us to God, being put to death in the flesh, but quickened by the Spirit" (I Pet. 3:18).

Inspired of God, Paul penned down these words: "Moreover, brethren, I declare unto you the Gospel which I preached unto you, which also ye have received, and wherein ye stand; by which also ye are saved, if ye keep in memory what I preached unto you, unless ye have believed in vain. For I delivered unto you first of all that which I also received, how that Christ died for our sins according to the Scriptures; and that He was buried, and that He rose again the third day according to the Scriptures" (I Cor. 15:1-4).

"For He hath made Him to be sin for us, who knew no sin; that we might be made the righteousness of God in Him" (II Cor. 5:21).

"Wherefore when He cometh into the world, He saith, Sacrifice and offering thou wouldest not, but a body hast thou prepared me" (Heb. 10:5).

". . . Without shedding of blood is no remission" (Heb. 9:22).

In John 3:36 we read, "He that believeth on the Son hath everlasting life: and he that believeth not the Son shall not see life; but the wrath of God abideth on him."

Again I ask, Did our Lord and Saviour Jesus Christ come into the world, suffer as He suffered, endure the torture and shame of the cross, just to make men moral? Or did He come to do *more* than that?

According to modern preaching, liberal theology, and today's anemic religion, the average person thinks that the Lord Jesus Christ came into the world to do good, to live a good life, to set a good example, to heal the sick, to comfort the sorrowing, to set up a standard of righteousness and live a life of thoughtful reverence and sincere devotion to the unseen God. But let me remind you that Jesus Christ was God Almighty in flesh! He did not come into the world to set standards or to be an example. *He came to bring salvation to hell-deserving sinners!*

Today, liberal, modernistic preachers are proclaiming that people should go about as Christ did, doing good, visiting the sick, taking care of the poor and the needy, being kind, gentle of manner, spreading sunshine in a dark world. These things are all commendable, to be sure, but beloved, such religion is not taught in the Word of God. Jesus Christ came into this world to do *more* than make men moral or spread sunshine in the darkness of man's day.

There are thousands of people on earth today who do not belong to any church, nor do they profess to be religious —but they are kind, benevolent, helpful, more or less cultured and refined, educated, living clean moral lives. These dear souls are respected and honored by their fellowman. Many of them are more generous than some church members are—they contribute large sums of money to good organizations. If we measure Christianity by these things,

10

then some folk who make no pretense of Christianity go much further than some who DO profess to be Christians.

But Christianity is NOT just clean living, liberal giving, good morals, or kindness toward our fellowman. *It is much, much more than these.* Salvation amounts to a great deal more than living a good life and doing good to others.

I am sure you want the Word of God on this subject, so we will use the Bible as our only textbook in this study of the new birth—the study of *immortality*, not morality; *redemption*, not clean living. We will look into the perfect law of liberty "that is able to make us wise unto salvation."

The Word of God is a lamp to our feet, a light to our pathway. The Word of God is not bound . . . the Word of God is quick and powerful, and sharper than any two-edged sword.

The Gospel is "the power of God unto salvation to everyone that believeth" (Rom. 1:16). To his converts James declares, "Of His own will begat He us with the word of truth, that we should be a kind of firstfruits of His creatures" (James 1:18). Peter cries out, "Being born again, not of corruptible seed, but of incorruptible, by the Word of God, which liveth and abideth for ever" (I Pet. 1:23). In Ephesians 2:8, 9 we read, "For by grace are ye saved through faith; and that not of yourselves: it is the gift of God: not of works, lest any man should boast." And Romans 10:17 tells us, ". . . Faith cometh by hearing, and hearing by the Word of God."

My dear friend, the only way any person can be saved is through the power of the Word of God. The only way any person can become clean—yea, clean and fit to enter the Pearly White City—is through the Word. In John 15:3

Jesus makes this statement: "Now ye are clean through the word which I have spoken unto you."

In II Timothy 1:9, 10 we read, "Who hath saved us, and called us with an holy calling, not according to our works, but according to His own purpose and grace, which was given us in Christ Jesus before the world began, but is now made manifest by the appearing of our Saviour Jesus Christ, who hath abolished death, and hath brought life and immortality to light through the Gospel."

"Who hath saved us . . ." This refers to God. God saves us, and He saves us for only one reason, as clearly set forth in Ephesians 4:32: ". . . Be ye kind one to another, tenderhearted, forgiving one another, even as God *for Christ's sake* hath forgiven you!"

In this marvelous verse of Scripture the Holy Spirit clearly says that God saves us FOR CHRIST'S SAKE. God did not save me because I was worthy of salvation, nor because I was fit to be saved—I was not *worth* saving! But Jesus purchased my redemption with His own precious blood, and because He died on the cross for sinners, God forgives for Christ's sake—and ONLY for Christ's sake. Apart from the shed blood of the Lord Jesus we cannot be saved, we cannot please God nor become His child.

"Who hath saved us, *and called us with an holy calling, not according to our works . . .*" According to God's Word we are not saved according to our works, we are not saved BY works—"not of works, lest any man should boast." All of the good works that we might do in a lifetime would not and could not atone for the least of our sins!

". . . But according to His own purpose and grace, which was given us in Christ Jesus before the world began . . ." We are not saved by works, but by the marvelous grace of

God—grace that was *provided* before God laid the foundation of the world.

"... *But is now made manifest by the appearing of our Saviour Jesus Christ* ..." This marvelous grace, this glorious salvation, though not revealed in the Old Testament era, is revealed—yea, has been brought down to man—by none other than the only begotten of the Father, very God in flesh! *Jesus was salvation* brought down to man.

And not only did Christ manifest salvation and light, but He *"abolished death and hath brought life and immortality to light through the Gospel."* The devil hates the Word of God; he despises the pure Gospel because it is through the Word and by the power of the Gospel that men are saved. It is utterly and absolutely impossible for any person to be saved until he *hears* the Word of God, *believes* the Word of God, *and receives the Christ* who WAS the Word in flesh.

In I Corinthians 15:1-4 Paul gives a clear outline of the Gospel—the death, burial, and resurrection of the Lord Jesus *"according to the Scriptures."* Paul did not preach salvation according to Judaism, Romanism, or any denominational belief. He preached the death, the burial, the resurrection of the Lord Jesus, and he preached according to the Scriptures.

It makes no difference what *you* think about the Word of God, nor what *I* think about it. It makes no difference what any minister *says* about it. The Word of God is forever settled in heaven (Psalm 119:89) and cannot be broken. The Word of God will face us when we stand to receive our just and due reward!

God saves us *for Christ's sake*—not according to our works, but according to His own purpose and grace. He

13

saves us through the finished work of Christ on Calvary —the work that was blueprinted by the Godhead before the foundation of this world.

Redemption was planned, provided, and perfected before this earth was created by Almighty God:

"Forasmuch as ye know that ye were not redeemed with corruptible things, as silver and gold, from your vain conversation received by tradition from your fathers; but with the precious blood of Christ, as of a lamb without blemish and without spot: Who verily was foreordained before the foundation of the world, but was manifest in these last times for you. Who by Him do believe in God, that raised Him up from the dead, and gave Him glory; that your faith and hope might be in God. Seeing ye have purified your souls in obeying the truth through the Spirit unto unfeigned love of the brethren, see that ye love one another with a pure heart fervently: being born again, not of corruptible seed, but of incorruptible, by the Word of God, which liveth and abideth for ever. For all flesh is as grass, and all the glory of man as the flower of grass. The grass withereth, and the flower thereof falleth away: But the Word of the Lord endureth for ever. And this is the Word which by the Gospel is preached unto you" (I Pet. 1:18-25).

In these verses we note that Peter and Paul agree one hundred percent concerning redemption. Peter declares,

". . . *Ye know that ye were not redeemed with corruptible things.*" Man has corrupted everything he has touched. All that is necessary for ruin to develop—in a child, a family, a community, or a nation—is simply for that child, that family, community, or nation to completely ignore God and His Word, make their own laws and run their own lives independent of God. In a few short years corruption will develop. Without God, man is helpless, hopeless, and hell-bound. Man can no more cleanse himself from sin and from his sinful nature than the leopard can change his spots.

I praise God for the comforting words of Peter. We are not redeemed with corruptible things! We have a redemption that is incorruptible and that will never fade away, because our redemption is *IN God, BY God, and THROUGH God.* Salvation does not come through anything that man's hands have provided or that man's wisdom has blueprinted.

We are redeemed *'with the precious blood of Christ, as of a lamb without blemish and without spot."* Jesus was the Lamb of God, and in Him there was no sin. He was the spotless One—pure, undefiled, untouched by sin. He who knew no sin was made sin that we might become the righteousness of God in Him. Jesus took upon Himself a body of flesh, a body like unto sinful man; and in that body He conquered every temptation hell hurled at Him. He overcame the world, the flesh, and the devil. He carried our sins to the cross and nailed them there! Hallelujah! We can shout the victory if we are covered by the precious blood of the Lamb!

". . . Who verily was foreordained before the foundation of the world, but was manifest in these last times for you." Before God ever laid the foundation of the world, before He created this universe, the Holy Trinity of God the Father, God the Son, and God the Holy Spirit held a conference and agreed that the Lamb would come into the world at the appointed time and pay the sin-debt. (Yes, I am a Trinitarian—I believe in one God manifest in three Persons. I could not believe the Bible and not believe in the Triune God.) All of this was planned and perfected before God created man, yea, in the eternity behind us *before the foundation of the world!*

15

This tremendous truth of salvation has been made manifest to us in these last days. We have been living in *the last days* ever since Jesus came to this earth to pay the sin-debt. These ARE the last days. In this day of grace, God is making His last loving, compassionate attempt to get men to serve HIM, live for Him, and honor Him as the only true God. These are the closing days of God's dealing with mankind. When the Church (the body of Christ) is completed, we will be caught up to meet Jesus in the air and this marvelous day of grace will come to a close.

God will then deal with earth's masses in terrible judgment. There will be souls saved during that time, but they will be saved by "enduring to the end"—that is, if they refuse to receive the mark of the beast, and instead of receiving his mark they surrender their lives to martyrdom, *they will be saved by enduring to the end.* And although a great multitude *will* be saved, they will not enjoy the marvelous salvation by grace as we enjoy it today.

The Bible clearly declares that when the Church is raptured, the Holy Spirit will be called out with the Church. Then it is that the 144,000 sealed ones, of the twelve tribes of Israel, will preach *the Gospel of the Kingdom.* These 144,000 missionaries will declare the coming of the King, and those who *accept* the message and refuse the mark of the beast will *enter* the kingdom. Those who *refuse* the message and follow the beast will be eternally damned. They cannot be forgiven after receiving the mark of the beast.

We are living in the most glorious days this world (and mankind) has ever known. Never has there been an age like this glorious age of grace—salvation by grace, through faith, *the gift of God.* Before God created man, *salvation* was planned and perfected; and in the fulness of time, Jesus

16

brought salvation down to man. He paid sin's debt with His own precious blood, and today He extends His nail-scarred hand to all who will come unto God by Him.

"Who by Him do believe in God, that raised Him up from the dead, and gave Him glory; that your faith and hope might be in God." Peter is preaching salvation by believing in God who raised up Jesus. Paul declared, ". . . If thou shalt confess with thy mouth the Lord Jesus, and shalt believe in thine heart that God hath raised Him from the dead, thou shalt be saved. For with the heart man believeth unto righteousness; and with the mouth confession is made unto salvation (Rom. 10:9, 10).

In our present verse, Peter preaches salvation by faith, in order that our faith and our hope might be in God—not in our works, our religion, or anything else that man can provide.. We are not saved by joining a church, we are not saved by baptism, we are not saved by good works. We are saved when we exercise faith in the finished work of Christ on the cross.

"Seeing ye have purified your souls in obeying the truth . . ." Beloved, what IS truth? In John 14:6 Jesus said to Thomas, "I am the Way, the Truth, and the Life." In John 8:32 he said, "Ye shall know the truth, and the truth shall make you free."

Jesus is truth, the Word is truth, and the Word and Jesus are inseparable because the Word of God is Christ, and Christ is the Word:

"In the beginning was the Word, and the Word was with God, and the Word was God . . . and the Word was made flesh, and dwelt among us" (John 1:1, 14 in part).

Notice that the Word tells us we purify our souls *in obeying the truth*—not in joining the church, not by being baptized in water, nor by daily living the best we know how. The Scripture does not tell us that we purify our souls by attending church, giving our money, or saying prayers. We purify our souls in obeying the truth—and the truth is the living Word of God! I repeat for emphasis, it is absolutely impossible for one to be born again apart from the Word of God.

I do not believe there is a verse in all of the Word of God that is any clearer or more easily understood than I Peter 1:23. We are born again—not of corruptible seed, but incorruptible—and the incorruptible seed is the Word of God, "which liveth and abideth for ever." Peter here is preaching the *"must"* of the new birth, the *"how"* of the new birth, the *result* of the new birth—and as Jesus taught Nicodemus, "Except a man be born again, he cannot see the kingdom of God."

I have repeatedly made the statement that apart from the Word of God it is impossible for one to be saved. The book of Acts gives us some very enlightening Scriptures along that line:

Just after Pentecost, five thousand were saved through the preaching of the Gospel (Acts 4:4).

The pure Gospel preached by Philip brought great revival in Samaria (Acts 8:5-8).

God called Philip to leave the revival in Samaria and journey south. On his journey he encountered the Ethiopian eunuch, and through expounding unto him the Word of God, he led the eunuch into salvation (Acts 8:26-39).

The jailer at Philippi cried out, "Sirs, what must I do to be saved?" Paul and Silas replied, "Believe on the Lord Jesus Christ, and thou shalt be saved, and thy house. *And*

18

they spake unto him the word of the Lord, and to all that were in his house" (Acts 16:25-34).

When Paul preached the Word of God in Ephesus, the Word proved to be the expeller of evil, and a mighty revival broke out (Acts 19:11-20).

In Acts 20:32 Paul says, "And now, brethren, I commend you to God, AND TO THE WORD OF HIS GRACE, WHICH IS ABLE TO BUILD YOU UP, AND TO GIVE YOU AN INHERITANCE AMONG ALL THEM WHICH ARE SANCTIFIED."

The Word of God is the answer for every need of every heart. The Word is alive, quick, powerful, sharper than any two-edged sword. It wounds to heal, and kills to make alive. The sure word of promise is a light to gladden our hearts and guide our footsteps. It harmonizes with all of man's needs, whether great or small.

In verses 24 and 25 of our passage from Peter, he tells us that all flesh is as grass, the glory of man is like the flower of the grass, which soon withers and the flowers fall away. And then by contrast he assures us that *"the Word of the Lord endureth for ever. And this is the Word which BY THE GOSPEL is preached unto you."* Peter preached nothing but the Word—the pure Gospel—because, like John, he had seen, touched, and bore witness to *the Living Word* (I John 1:1-3). He knew the risen, living Saviour . . . Peter preached the blood, he preached the new birth through faith in the finished work of Christ our Lord. Redemption comes through the blood, and apart from the shedding of blood there is no remission for sin. The new birth comes through the power of the Gospel, and apart from the Gospel there IS no new birth.

Writing to Titus, his son n the ministry, Paul says, "For

we ourselves also were sometimes foolish, disobedient, deceived, serving divers lusts and pleasures, living in malice and envy, hateful, and hating one another. But after that the kindness and love of God our Saviour toward man appeared, not by works of righteousness which we have done, but according to His mercy He saved us, by the washing of regeneration, and renewing of the Holy Ghost; which He shed on us abundantly through Jesus Christ our Saviour; that being justified by His grace, we should be made heirs according to the hope of eternal life" (Tit. 3:3-7).

Paul clearly teaches that *all unbelievers* are disobedient to God, deceived, serving all kinds of lusts and worldly pleasures, living in malice and envy, hateful, and hating each other. You will note that he says, *"WE ourselves,"* thus putting himself in the same category. (He is, of course, referring to the time before his conversion.)

He paints a hideous word-picture of the unbeliever— and then—*"After that the kindness and love of God our Saviour toward man appeared . . ."* Beloved, God loved us while we were yet unlovely! We were not fit to be loved, we were not worthy of His love; but He loved us even before He made the world. He loved us *so much* that He agreed to the death of Jesus on the cross, that we, through faith in His finished work, might escape eternity in hell— and make no mistake, my friend, there IS a hell! The hottest sermon ever delivered on the subject of hell was preached by none other than the tender Lamb of God, who died on the cross to save us FROM hell. Read Mark 9:42-48.

In Titus 3:5 Paul gives a beautiful outline of salvation —clear and concise; and you will note that he does not say one word about moral living. He *does* say, *"Not by works of righteousness which we have done."* All of the good works we could do and all of the right living we could live would only add up to "filthy rags" in the sight of God (Isa. 64:6).

"But according to HIS MERCY He saved us . . ." Note, first of all, His *mercy*. Beloved, never rush into God's presence and demand *justice*. If I had justice I would be in hell today! I live, I enjoy the abundance of God's blessings and the favor of His grace—not because I deserve it, but because He has been exceedingly merciful to me—and I know He has been merciful to YOU. I am what I am by the grace of God. I am saved today because of His shed blood. God saved me for Jesus' sake the night I put my trust in the finished work of the Saviour.

". . . By the washing of regeneration, and the renewing of the Holy Ghost." Paul did not say, "by the washing of the baptistry," nor did he say "by the merit of good, clean, moral living." He said, "By the washing of regeneration"— and regeneration comes through the Word of God. We are clean through the Word. The Holy Spirit convicts us, draws us, and baptizes us into the body of Christ when we are born of the Spirit and washed in the blood.

In the book of Genesis, the blood began to flow. Adam and Eve deliberately disobeyed God by eating the forbidden fruit. Then they immediately set about to prepare a covering for the shame of their nakedness—they sewed fig leaves together and made aprons for themselves.

Everything was fine until—*"they heard the voice of the Lord God walking in the garden in the cool of the day:* and Adam and his wife hid themselves from the presence of the Lord God amongst the trees of the garden."

God called out, "Adam . . . where art thou?" Adam cried out in fear from his hiding place among the trees; and when God asked him what he had done, he of course laid all the blame on Eve, and Eve in turn blamed the serpent. But God

21

did not accept their excuses—nor did He accept their coverings.

God slew innocent animals, and at the price of the blood of those animals He made coats for Adam and Eve. Thus we have the first blood covering, and since that day when God covered Adam and Eve at the price of the shed blood of the innocent animals, there has been no covering *apart* from the blood of the innocent sacrifice of the Lamb of God.

Rivers of blood flowed from Genesis to Malachi. Tens of thousands of animals, doves, and pigeons were slain and their blood was offered on the altar. But in Hebrews 10:1-6 Paul declares:

"For the law having a shadow of good things to come, and not the very image of the things, can never with those sacrifices which they offered year by year continually make the comers thereunto perfect. For then would they not have ceased to be offered? Because that the worshippers once purged should have had no more conscience of sins. But in those sacrifices there is a remembrance again made of sins every year. For it is not possible that the blood of bulls and of goats should take away sins. Wherefore when He cometh into the world, He saith, Sacrifice and offering thou wouldest not, *but a body thou hast prepared me:* In burnt-offerings and sacrifices for sin thou hast had no pleasure."

Beloved, every innocent animal slain in the Old Testament era pointed to the blood of the Lamb of God, fore-ordained before the foundation of the world. His blood, shed on Calvary, made good the offerings of those in the Old Testament who, in faith, offered blood on the altar. Had not Jesus died on the cross, the blood shed throughout the Old Testament era would have been shed in vain, and those

22

who offered it would have died without hope and their spirits would be tormented in the pits of the damned!

The blood of the Lord Jesus Christ, God's Son, cleanses from ALL sin. The Old Testament Christian looked *forward* to Calvary, the New Testament Christian *looks back* to Calvary, where Jesus, on the cross, settled the sin-debt for ALL, forever. He offered His blood once, to be offered no more. Therefore there remains no sacrifice for sin. We must either put our faith in the shed blood of Jesus, or suffer the eternal torment of a devil's hell. Apart from the blood of the Lord Jesus Christ, there is no covering, no remission, no forgiveness for sin.

"... *A body thou hast prepared me.*" What the law could not do because of the weakness of the flesh, God accomplished when He gave His only begotten Son in a body *like unto* sinful flesh, and in that body He condemned sin in the flesh (Rom. 8:1-4).

"But we see Jesus, who was made a little lower than the angels for the suffering of death, crowned with glory and honour; that He by the grace of God should taste death for every man" (Heb. 2:9).

This verse gives a very clear statement concerning Jesus—how and why He came into the world. Notice that He was made "a little lower" than the angels. He did not take a body like unto the angels, but like unto sinful man, in order that He might suffer, and die. He DID suffer death, and He is now crowned with glory and honor.

Jesus came into the world "that He, *by the grace of God,* should taste death for every man." Had it not been for God's grace, He would never have allowed Jesus to suffer the terrible death of the cross. Christ did not come into the world to make men moral, or to make men good, nor

23

to clean up lives and cities. He came into this world, took a body like unto the body of sinful flesh, that He might suffer and die, that He might taste the bitter dregs of death, *for every man.*

"For Christ also hath once *suffered for sins,* the just for the unjust, that He might bring us to God, being put to death in the flesh, but quickened by the Spirit" (I Pet. 3:18). Beloved, do you see the sinless Son of God as He suffers—He who knew no sin, but was made to be sin for us? Can you imagine the agony of His Suffering? Is it possible for the finite mind to even *think* of His suffering? Consider that the sinner's place is in hell; and *since Jesus took the sinner's place* He suffered all the agony, all the woe, all the torment and sorrow of an everlasting hell—the Just suffering for the unjust, that He might bring us to God!

He did not suffer that He might make us moral, or that He might make us good, or that He might make us religious. He suffered that He might bring us to God—and it *took* all the pain and agony He endured to keep you and me out of hell! By like token, those who refuse to receive Him, those who refuse to trust in His finished work, will suffer in hell all that HE suffered to keep them OUT of hell!

I want us to hear the testimony of the Holy Spirit as the Word of God gives it to us in the Gospels. First, let us hear Matthew:

"Then cometh Jesus with them unto a place called Gethsemane, and saith unto the disciples, Sit ye here, while I go and pray yonder. And He took with Him Peter, and the two sons of Zebedee, and began to be sorrowful and very heavy. Then saith He unto them, *My soul is exceeding sorrowful, even unto death:* Tarry ye here, and watch with me" (Matt. 26:36-68).

24

The Garden of Gethsemane was a place where Jesus often went to pray. Matthew tells us that on this occasion the Saviour cried out, "My soul is exceeding sorrowful, even unto death!" In other words, He said, *"My soul is about to die!"* Jesus was literally pouring out His soul for sin. Beloved, get this: JESUS TOOK THE SINNER'S PLACE— and the sinner's place is in an eternal hell. That is what God declares in His word: *"The soul that sinneth, it shall die . . ."* (Ezek. 18:20). *"The wages of sin is death . . ."* (Rom. 6:23). *". . . Sin, when it is finished, bringeth forth death"* (James 1:15). Sin and death are synonymous.

Is it possible for us to imagine the agony of that hour when Jesus cried out, "My soul is exceeding sorrowful, even unto death"? And yet, that hour was imperative, as we will see a bit later in our study. It was absolutely necessary that Jesus suffer the agony He described in that prayer!

Now let us hear *Mark's* testimony as the Holy Spirit speaks through Him: "And they came to a place which was named Gethsemane: and He saith to His disciples, Sit ye here, while I shall pray. And He taketh with Him Peter and James and John, and began to be sore amazed, and to be very heavy; and saith unto them, *My soul is exceeding sorrowful unto death:* tarry ye here, and watch" (Mark 14:32-34).

What do we find in Mark's account that Matthew did not tell us? Mark declares that Jesus *"began to be sore AMAZED."* Scholars tell us that the Greek work used here is the same as that used in Mark 16:5 where the Spirit describes the women as being *affrighted* (or terrified).

According to God's Word, Jesus was present when God the Father threw Satan out of heaven and cast down the disobedient angels with him. He witnessed the flood in Noah's day, when every living creature (save Noah and his family) was destroyed. He witnessed the ground opening and swallowing up "all the men that appertained unto Korah . . . they went down alive into the pit" (Num. 16:32, 33). He sat in heaven's glory and saw the burning of Sodom and Gomorrah.

Beloved, I ask you, in the name of all that is high and holy, if Jesus saw all of these sights of torture and torment without amazement or fright, *then what did He see in the Garden of Gethsemane that sorely amazed and terrified Him?* Surely there are not enough words in all the languages of all the world to describe the agony through which He passed in that hour!

Personally, I believe He saw the devil and all hell marshalled against Him to stop Him. Satan knew that the shed blood of Christ on the cross meant sure defeat for him; and if you will make a careful study of the Old Testament you will discover that from Genesis to Malachi a river of blood flowed as the devil attempted to stop the seed of the woman whom God Almighty informed him would bruise his head. I believe that Jesus saw all the emissaries of hell, the powers of spiritual wickedness, marshalled in all their strength against Him. He saw the cup that contained all the bitter dregs of sin—and He saw these things *in the flesh* as He had never seen them before. The scene was so much more horrible, so much more terrifying, when He saw it through the eyes of the flesh, that the sight amazed and terrified Him. Beloved, *the sinless Son of God suffered all this—and more—that you and I might be saved!*

Now let us hear the testimony of *Luke* concerning the suffering of our Lord:

"And He came out, and went, as He was wont, to the mount of Olives; and His disciples also followed Him. And when He was at the place, He said unto them, Pray that ye

26

enter not into temptation. And He was withdrawn from them about a stone's cast, and kneeled down, and prayed, saying, Father, if thou be willing, remove this cup from me: Nevertheless not my will, but thine, be done. *And there appeared an angel unto Him from heaven, strengthening Him. And being in an agony He prayed more earnestly: and His sweat was as it were great drops of blood falling down to the ground.* And when He rose up from prayer, and was come to His disciples, He found them sleeping for sorrow, and said unto them, Why sleep ye? Rise and pray, lest ye enter into temptation" (Luke 22:39-46).

What does Luke point out that Matthew and Mark did not tell us? He tells us that in this terrible agony, Jesus prayed so earnestly that His sweat became "as it were great drops of blood!" I am sure that all who read these lines know that Luke was a physician—and who would detect bloody perspiration more quickly than a doctor? Luke points out that as Jesus knelt and prayed, His suffering was so terrible that the arteries in His body, the veins in His face —yea, the smallest vessels in His hands, were so energized in agony that they began to shed forth His atoning blood!

But beloved, Jesus did not come into this world to spill His blood in the Garden of Gethsemane. It was imperative that His blood be shed on the cross. Satan's struggle against the sacrifice of the Lamb of God was so great that he attempted to shed His precious blood *before* He reached Calvary—as He lay prostrate on the ground in the agony of prayer! But God sent an angel from heaven to lift up and strengthen the Saviour.

We have considered the testimony of Matthew, Mark, and Luke. Now let us listen to John the Beloved as he records the words of Jesus:

"Now is my soul troubled; and what shall I say? Father,

27

save me from this hour: but for this cause came I unto this hour. Father, glorify thy name. Then came there a voice from heaven, saying, I have both glorified it, and will glorify it again. The people therefore, that stood by, and heard it, said that it thundered:others said, An angel spake to Him. Jesus answered and said, This voice came not because of me, but for your sakes. Now is the judgment of this world: now shall the prince of this world be cast out. *And I, if I be lifted up from the earth, will draw all men unto me. This He said, signifying what death He should die"* (John 12:27-33).

Nowhere does John refer to the Lord's perspiration being stained with blood, nor to the fact that Jesus was sorely amazed, nor that He was exceeding heavy and sorrowful. But he gives us the words of Jesus as He faces the hour when He will taste death for every man.

Jesus cried out, "What shall I say? Shall I say, Father, save me from this hour?" Then He answers, "No, I dare not say, Father, save me from this hour, because *I came into the world* for this very hour, this hour when I shall taste death for every man, this hour when I shall battle and conquer all hell for all who will accept my finished work!"

Now beloved, is it to be supposed that Jesus left the glories of heaven, stepped from the bosom of the Father to the manger in a stable, gave up the riches of glory for the poverty of His earthly ministry, just for the sake of setting an example? Did He suffer all of the agony of Gethsemane, plus the humiliation of His trial, the scourging, the plucking out of his beard by the roots, the piercing of His brow with the crown of thorns, the buffeting and the mocking of the crowds, just to make men moral? In the words of Isaiah, was He wounded, bruised, chastened, smitten, and crucified on a Roman cross—just to make sober men out of drunk-

28

ards, ladies out of harlots, and honest men out of thieves? Did He suffer the shame of the cross that we might become respectable citizens and clean-living people?

The Word of God gives the answer. Christ did NOT endure all of the agony, sorrow, heartbreak and humiliation that was heaped upon Him simply that we might become moral beings and make this world a better place to live in. Until the very moment when He said, "It is finished!" and passed His spirit back to God, all that He did, all that He said, all that He suffered was *in order that you and I might be born again and have within our bosom the Spirit of the living God!*

Through the miracle of the new birth we poor, finite creatures have the divine nature of the eternal God—and that miracle is made possible ONLY as we believe in the shed blood, the death, burial, and resurrection of the Lord Jesus, *according to the Scriptures.*

We do not hear much about the suffering of Jesus in this age of anemic, "sissy" religion. Too many sermons today are bloodless, void of the message of suffering. Today we hear a gospel that detours around the cross, a gospel that is without suffering, without blood, and without repentance.

It is not surprising that some preachers preach only once a week—and only a twenty-minute sermonette, at that! When a minister detours around the virgin birth, the blood atonement, the sufferings of Christ at Calvary, repentance for sin, and the verbal inspiration of the Bible, and confines his sermon to "the fatherhood of God and the brotherhood of man," it is understandable that it takes him six days of the week to prepare his sermonette for Sunday morning! It would take *me* many long hours, I am sure, to prepare a sermon from a social Gospel—but beloved, by the

29

grace of God and as much as in me is, *I will preach the Gospel of the cross*—the "bloody" Gospel, if you please—*until the Lord Jesus calls me home!*

My Bible tells me that without the shedding of blood is no remission for sin. It tells me that we are redeemed —not with corruptible things, but with the precious blood of the Lamb of God. It tells me that the blood of Jesus Christ, God's Son, cleanses from all sin. And as it was in the land of Egypt the night the death angel passed through, so it is today. God is still saying, "When I see the *blood,* I will pass over you!"

I am convinced that this side of heaven we will never know the power of the Word of God. Please turn to the eighteenth chapter of John's Gospel, and read the first eleven verses. You will note that a band of men and soldiers, led by Judas, came to the garden to arrest the Lord. They came with lanterns, and torches, and weapons. Jesus, knowing all things, asked them, "Whom seek ye?" They replied, "Jesus of Nazareth." Jesus then said unto them, "I AM HE"—and they "went backward, and fell to the ground!" What I want to point out here is *the power of the Word.* Jesus very calmly spoke three words—*"I am He"*—and the power of those words flattened His enemies to the ground.

But I can assure you that if you will *receive the Word,* it is the power of God unto salvation. If you *reject* the Word, you will be judged by the Word in the last day. Jesus said, "He that rejecteth me, and receiveth not my words, hath one that judgeth him: the WORD that I have spoken, *the same shall judge him in the last day"* (John 12:48). If you will receive the Word, it is the power of God unto the salvation of your soul; but if you hear and *reject* the Word, woe be unto you when the power of that Word falls upon you in judgment!

I am aware that the minister who dares preach the blood today is branded "a slaughterhouse preacher," but I must preach the whole truth of the Gospel, and I know that the blood is what will determine a soul's eternal destiny. If you are covered by the blood, you will hear God say, "Enter thou into the joys of thy Lord." If you are NOT covered by the blood, you will hear Him say, "Take him away—bind him—and cast him into everlasting darkness, where there is weeping and wailing and gnashing of teeth!"

Before going further in the message, let me ask you— Are YOU saved? Do you KNOW that you are born again? Do you know that you are covered with the shed blood of the Lord Jesus Christ? Can you sing, "Blessed assurance, Jesus is mine! Oh, what a foretaste of glory divine"? When a minister asks you, "Are you saved?" do you reply, "I am a church member . . . I have been baptized . . . I live the very best I know how"?

If that is the way you answer the all-important salvation question, then I beg you to get on your knees NOW and call on God. Ask Him to save you for Christ's sake. Put your faith in the shed blood of His cross. If you are hoping in church membership, good works, good living, or morality, you HAVE no hope—you are lost! The Bible clearly declares, "Ye MUST be born again . . . Except ye repent, ye shall perish." If you are not born again, bow your head, receive the Lord Jesus Christ, and He will save you this very moment.

CHAPTER II

The Gospel—The Power of God Unto Salvation

Paul tells us that all Scripture is given by inspiraton, and that all Scripture is profitable unto us (II Tim. 3:16, 17), but he also admonishes us to study to show ourselves approved unto God, that we may rightly divide the word of truth (II Tim. 2:15).

All Scripture IS inspired, all Scripture is God's Word—but each book in the Bible has a specific message, and every book in the Bible has a key that unlocks that book.

Some have asked, "Why do we have four Gospels?" The answer is recorded IN the Gospels:

Matthew is "the book of the generation of Jesus Christ, the Son of David, the son of Abraham" (Matt. 1:1). You will note here that Matthew connects Jesus with two of the most important of all Old Testament covenants: The Davidic covenant of kinship, and the Abrahamic covenant of promise (II Sam. 7:8-16; Gen. 15:18). He writes of Jesus as King, the son of David, and also as the son of Abraham, obedient unto death according to the Isaac type (Gen. 22:1-18; Heb. 11:8-19). He presents Jesus as King of the Jews, the covenanted King.

Matthew is primarily the Gospel for Israel—until the death of Jesus Christ, after which it becomes a Gospel for the whole world.

Mark presents Jesus as the mighty Worker, Jehovah's servant, the Branch (Zech. 3:8), the One who came into the world to lay down His life for poor, lost sinners; and throughout the Gospel of Mark the *servant* character of the incarnate Son is manifest. The key-verse is Mark 10:45: "For even the Son of man came not to be ministered unto,

33

but to minister, and to give His life a ransom for many."

Luke presents the Saviour as the human-Divine One. The key-verse is Luke 19:10: "For the Son of man is come to seek and to save that which was lost."

In contrast to Luke, *John's* Gospel presents Jesus as the Divine-human One, the incarnate, eternal Word, the Son of God—yea, *God in flesh*. The key that unlocks this glorious book is found in John 20:30, 31: "And many other signs truly did Jesus in the presence of His disciples, which are not written in this book: But these are written, that ye might believe that Jesus is the Christ, the Son of God; and that believing ye might have life through His name!"

The last verse in John's Gospel is interesting: "And there are also many other things which Jesus did, the which, if they should be written every one, I suppose that even the world itself could not contain the books that should be written. Amen." In other words, Jesus did so much during His earthly ministry that books could never contain the account of all that He did. But John's Gospel is recorded for a specific purpose—that we might believe that Jesus is the Christ, and, believing that Jesus is the Christ, have life through His name. The Gospel of John was written to point us to Christ for salvation, to instruct us *how* to be saved, and to enlighten us in the *simplicity* of this glorious salvation.

Since the Gospel of John is the salvation book, we will spend the rest of our time studying the ministry of the Lord Jesus Christ as recorded there. In John 1:10-13 we find these words:

"He was in the world, and the world was made by Him, and the world knew Him not. He came unto His own, and His own received Him not. But as many as received Him,

34

to them gave He power to become the sons of God, even to them that believe on His name: Which were born, not of blood, nor of the will of the flesh, nor of the will of man, but of God."

These verses contain several interesting truths:

1. In verse 10, Jesus was in the world, a world that was made BY HIM, and yet the world did not know or recognize Him.

2. In verse 11, Jesus came "unto His own"—(which in this instance refers to Israel, God's chosen people)—but they did not receive Him. They cried out, "We will not have this man to reign over us! Crucify Him! We want Barabbas, the robber. Crucify Jesus of Nazareth, and let His blood be upon us and upon our children!!" And certainly in our day we have seen the children of Israel butchered by the millions. Not only was *the world* in total ignorance concerning the Lord Jesus, but even His own people did not recognize Him as their Messiah.

3. In verse 12, to "as many as received Him" He gave the power to become sons of God. They did not *merit* the power, they did not *purchase* the power, they did not *pray down* the power. Jesus GAVE them the power to become sons of God when they believed on His name.

4. In verse 13, we learn that those who received Him were *born* into the family of God. Beloved, we do not "join" Jesus, we do not "join" Christianity, we do not "join" salvation. *We are BORN into God's family.* Salvation comes as the result of a birth, and birth denotes *life*. To all who receive Jesus, He gives the power to be born—but this birth is not of (human) blood, the blood of our ancestors; it is not of the will of the flesh, no matter how royal our ancestry may be; nor is it according to the will of man. The new birth is OF GOD!

35

What John, through the Holy Spirit, is attempting to drive home to our hearts is the Bible fact that *salvation is of the Lord, by the power of Almighty God.* Dear reader, we can no more save ourselves than we can "born" ourselves into *physical* existence. We owe our physical existence to our parents, for they gave us physical life. The same is true in the spiritual realm. If we are born again, we are born again because we received the power of God by faith. We are born again through the power of the Gospel, the living Word—and those who are NOT born of God are lost and on their way to hell!

Acts 4:12 tells us plainly, "Neither is there salvation in any other: for there is none other name under heaven given among men, whereby we must be saved."

Beloved, the only way lost humanity can be saved is through the power of God. When we recognize our need of a Saviour, when we believe on the Lord Jesus Christ as the virgin-born Son of God, crucified, buried, and risen, God "borns" us into the family of heaven. We do not "join" God's family—we are BORN into it. Church membership has never saved anyone, and never will. The water in the baptistry has never saved anyone, and never will. Good, clean, moral living has never saved anyone, and never will. Even sincere religious activity has never saved anyone, and never will. GOD saves us, according to His own will and purpose by gracee, when we exercise faith in the death, burial, and resurrection of the Son of God.

As time and space permit, we will study several individuals who came to the Lord Jesus and were saved by Him during His earthly ministry. One of the most interesting of these individuals is Nicodemus. You will find the account of his conversion in the third chapter of John. It would be well to read the entire chapter—it is too lengthy to be

36

quoted here in its entirety.

In John 3:1 we learn that Nicodemus was an upstanding, outstanding person. He was not a slum-bum in the gutter on the street of forgotten men. He was a Pharisee—and that means that he was religious. He was a ruler of the Jews, which signifies that he had the respect of the people, in that he was appointed to a position of authority. But this religionist, this educated, respected Pharisee, had a hunger in his heart. He had heard of this Teacher named Jesus—perhaps he had heard reports both pro and con. Perhaps some had praised the Master to the highest degree while others had criticized Him and called Him an imposter. But Nicodemus decided to find out for himself if this unusual Teacher could satisfy the need of his heart.

John 3:2 tells us that Nicodemus came to Jesus by night. WHY he came under cover of darkness is not stated in the Scripture. Some have suggested that Nicodemus was afraid of the Jews, and therefore dared not come to see Jesus of Nazareth in the daytime. Others have said that perhaps he was *too busy* during the daylight hours, and thus of necessity sought the Saviour after business hours. Whatever the reason for his coming to Jesus by night, the *important* thing is that he CAME—and found salvation for his soul.

He opened his conversation with Jesus by saying, *"Rabbi, we know that thou art a teacher come from God: for no man can do these miracles that thou doest, except God be with him."* This verse is very precious. Nicodemus was not a skeptic, he was not a critic. He had a hungry heart, and he recognized in Jesus a power that only God could supply. Nicodemus *believed* in the power of God— (which is more than can be said for some of the outstanding theologians of our day)!

37

I do not know what kind of an answer Nicodemus expected from the lips of Jesus; but the answer he received was very direct, almost abrupt. Jesus said, *"Verily, verily, I say unto thee, Except a man be born again, he cannot see the Kingdom of God."*

Our modern theologians would not have been so abrupt. They would have gently led Nicodemus. After the great compliment he had just paid Jesus, it would seem to them 'that *at least* the Lord might have said, "Thank you, Dr. Nicodemus. I understand that you are quite an outstanding personality, yourself. I hear that you are a Pharisee, a ruler among the Jews, a master in religion." But that is not what Jesus said. In spite of the fact that Nicodemus was a master in Israel, he immediately instructed him that he must be born again if he hoped to see the kingdom of God.

Beloved, it matters not how good a church member you may be, nor to what denomination you belong. Accordng to the words of Jesus, *"Except a man be born again, he cannot see the kingdom of God."*

I like the wording of the Bible—there are no loopholes there. Scriptures leave no untied ends. Jesus said *"a man,"* and that means ALL men, EVERY man. All have sinned and come short of the glory of God, and the wages of sin is death. We must ALL be born again if we hope to see or enter the kingdom of God.

Nicodemus then asked a question—a very natural question, one that indicates his sincerity. He had not come to Jesus for the purpose of criticizing Him; he had an emptiness in his heart, and he was earnestly, sincerely,seeking truth. He asked, "How can a man be born when he is old?. Can he enter the second time into his mother's womb, and be born?" Like so many good people today, Nicodemus was thinking in terms of the flesh—but Jesus was talking about a *spiritual* birth.

In answer to the question of Nicodemus, Jesus replied, "Verily, verily, I say unto thee, Except a man be born of water and of the Spirit, he cannot enter into the kingdom of God. That which is born of the flesh is flesh; and that which is born of the Spirit is spirit."

When Jesus said, "Except a man be born of water," was He referring to water baptism—immersion in the River Jordan or in a baptistry? Remember—God gives the power of birth, and it is not *flesh* that is born again, but *spirit*. Since God GIVES the power of birth, and since the new birth has to do with the spirit and not with the flesh, could the water in a baptistry—or in any other place—reach the spirit to 'born" it or to cleanse it from sin? No, beloved— the "water" of John 3:5 is NOT water in a baptistry, nor in the river Jordan. The "water" to which Jesus refers, the water that "borns" us into God's family, is THE WORD OF GOD. If there were any place in the Word of God where I could read, "Except a man be immersed in water, he cannot enter the kingdom of God," then I would preach baptism as essential to salvation; but the Bible does not say that.

In John 5:24 we read: "Verily, verily, I say unto you, He that heareth my word, and believeth on Him that sent me, hath everlasting life, and shall not come into codemnation; but is passed from death unto life."

To His disciples Jesus said, "Now ye are clean through the Word which I have spoken unto you" (John 15:3).

To the church at Ephesus Paul wrote, "Husbands, love your wives, *even as Christ also loved the Church, and gave Himself for it;* that He might sanctify and cleanse it WITH THE WASHING OF WATER BY THE WORD, that He

39

might present it to himself a glorious Church, not having spot, or wrinkle, or any such thing; but that it should be holy and without blemish . . . This is a great mystery: but I speak concerning Christ and the Church" (Eph. 5:25-32 in part).

The only way to become a member of THE Church is to be born again. In Acts 2:47 we are told that the Lord added to the Church daily such as were being saved. He adds to the Church all who believe and are born again—and HE gives the power of birth. The believer is sanctified and cleansed "with the washing of the water BY THE WORD."

Peter sheds light on this subject. In I Peter 1:23 he declares, "Being born again, not of corruptible seed, but of incorruptible, *by the Word of God*, which liveth and abideth for ever." This verse clearly states that the new birth comes through and by the Word of God, it does not come through the baptistry. The baptistry is not "the seed" spoken of here.

When Jesus said to Nicodemus, "Except a man be born of water and of the Spirit, he cannot enter the kingdom of God, he was simply saying, "Except you receive the living water, the water that gushed from the rock when Moses struck it, you cannot enter the kingdom of God. Nicodemus, you are a master in Israel, you are well versed in the religion of the Jews—and you should know that the rock which Moses struck was a type of the Christ. You should know that the water which gushed from the rock was a type of the Living Water that came down from heaven. Since you are a master in the religion of Israel, you should recognize, by my miracles and through my words, that I am the Water of Life. I am the Rock which the builders rejected—but I have become the Chief Cornerstone. Nicodemus, you must

40

be born of water—the Living Water. You must receive my Word and be transformed by the power of the Holy Spirit, or you *cannot enter* the kingdom of God."

Paul was God's ordained minister to the Gentiles, and God Almighty honored Paul in that He dictated thirteen of the New Testament epistles to him. Certainly we should be willing to hear the words of that great apostle. In I Corinthians 1:17 he said, "... *Christ sent me not to baptize, but to preach the Gospel:* not with wisdom of words, lest the cross of Christ should be made of none effect."

Hear this man again: "For BY GRACE are ye saved through faith; and that not of yourselves: it is the gift of God: not of works, lest any man should boast" (Eph. 2:8, 9).

In Romans 10:9, 10 he said, "... If thou shalt confess with thy mouth the Lord Jesus, and shalt believe in thine heart that God hath raised Him from the dead, thou shalt be saved. For with the heart man believeth unto righteousness; and with the mouth confession is made unto salvation." In Titus 3:5 he proclaimed, "Not by works of righteousness which we have done, *but according to His mercy He saved us, by the washing of regeneration, and renewing of the Holy Ghost.*"

Beloved, let us be reasonable: If water baptism is essential to salvation, would the apostle to the Gentiles have said, "Christ sent me NOT to baptize, but to preach the Gospel"? If baptism were fifty percent of the new birth, Paul would have *preached* baptism as essential to salvation! But salvation is of God—by grace, through faith, *plus nothing.*

Let me make it clear that I believe in water baptism. I have been baptized, and I believe that every born again child of God should follow Christ in baptism. But the New

41

Testament teaches baptism FOR Christians—not baptism to make (or help to make) one a Christian. Baptism is a testimony that we have died to sin, we are buried with Christ, and raised to walk in newness of life. It is the cleansing of the shed blood, the washing of regeneration, that saves us; it is not the washing of the flesh in a baptistry.

Suppose we let Paul give us the outline of salvation: "For whosoever shall call upon the name of the Lord shall be saved. How then shall they CALL on Him in whom they have not BELIEVED? And how shall they believe in Him of whom they have not HEARD? And how shall they hear without a PREACHER? And how shall they preach, except they be SENT? . . . So then faith cometh by hearing, and hearing by the Word of God" (Rom. 10:13-17 in part).

We might say this is the plan of salvation in reverse. In verse 17 the Word of God brings faith—the first essential of salvation. We are saved by grace, but saving grace becomes ours through faith. But the Word cannot bring faith until the preacher *preaches* the Word (vv 14, 15). The sinner *hears* the Word, and hearing, he *believes* the Word. He then calls upon the name of the Lord Jesus and is saved. Hearing the Word brings faith, in faith the sinner calls, and *God saves*. If baptism were necessary for salvation, why did not Paul tell us so in this marvelous outline of salvation?

John 4:6-39 gives the account of a precious woman who, though very sinful, was gloriously saved, and in her city she turned many people to the Lord. This woman was saved through the living water. She asked Jesus for a drink, and He gave her living water. What did He give her? He gave her *His words*—seven words: "I that speak unto thee am HE" (John 4:26). She asked for living water, Jesus gave her the Word. She believed those words, and leaving her waterpot she ran to town, proclaiming, "Come, see a man, which told me all things that ever I did: Is not this the Christ? . . . And many of the Samaritans of that city believed on Him for the saying of the woman . . ." (John 4:29, 39). When Jesus said, "Except a man be born of water" He was referring to the living water—the Word of God. Actually, He was referring to Himself, because He was the Word in flesh, full of grace and truth (John 1:1, 14).

Now let us look at the part the SPIRIT plays in the new birth. Jesus said, "Except a man be born of water AND of the SPIRIT, he cannot enter into the kingdom of God."

The Holy Spirit draws men to God. In John 6:44 we read, No man can come to me, except the Father which hath sent me draw him . . ." In John 16:7-11 Jesus told His disciples, "Nevertheless I tell you the truth; it is expedient for you that I go away; for if I go not away, the Comforter will not come unto you; but if I depart, I will send Him unto you. And when He is come, He will reprove the world of sin, and of righteousness, and of judgment: Of sin, because they believe not on me: Of righteousness, because I go to my Father, and ye see me no more: Of judgment, because the prince of this world is judged."

According to these words of Jesus, it was necessary that He depart this earth, for if He did *not* depart, the Comforter (the Holy Spirit) would not come. We know that the Holy Spirit DID come on the Day of Pentecost, and He has been in the world ever since that day—reproving, convicting, warning of judgment, teaching us, and drawing sinners to God.

In I Corinthians 12:12-14 we read, "For as the body is

one, and hath many members, and all the members of that one body, being many, are one body: so also is Christ. For by ONE SPIRIT are we all baptized into one body, whether we be Jews or Gentiles, whether we be bond or free; and have been all made to drink into ONE SPIRIT. For the body is not one member, but many."

Here is the clear teaching concerning the Spirit's work when we exercise faith in God through our Lord Jesus Christ. When we hear the Word and realize our need of a Saviour, we *believe* the Word, and the Holy Spirit draws us to repentance. When we repent with a true heart and believe on the Lord Jesus Christ, that very second the Holy Spirit baptizes us into the *body* of Christ. But that is not the end of the ministry of the Holy Spirit.

We know that the Holy Spirit convicts us of sin and draws us to Christ. He is the attending physician at the spiritual birth. He baptizes us into the body of Christ— and then takes up His abode in the heart of the believer: "If any man have not the Spirit of Christ, he is none of His" (Rom. 8:9 b). II Peter 1:4 declares, "Whereby are given unto us exceeding great and precious promises: that by these ye might be partakers of the divine nature, having escaped the corruption that is in the world through lust." There is absolutely no such thing as Christianity apart from the Holy Spirit, for He abides in the bosom of every born again child of God.

The Holy Spirit not only abides—He FILLS all believers who will permit Him to fill their hearts and lives. In Ephesians 5:18 Paul says, ". . . Be not drunk with wine, wherein is excess; *but be filled with the Spirit.*" The Holy Spirit will not fully possess and fill us if we are not first willing to allow the Lord Jesus to *empty* us of all selfishness, pride, ALL things of the flesh. When we are willing to be entirely emptied, then the Holy Spirit is ready, willing, and anxious to fill us. But He does more: He is our *Guide*.

In Romans 8:14 we read, "For as many as are led by the Spirit of God, they are the sons of God." According to that verse of Scripture, if you are not led by the Spirit of God you are *not God's child;* and by like token, if you *are* God's child, you are led by the Holy Spirit!

David did not know this particular verse of Scripture as we have it today, but he cried out, "The Lord is my Shepherd . . . *He leadeth me* in the paths of righteousness (right living) for His name's sake." The same is true today in this dispensation of grace.

The Holy Spirit also gives us assurance: "The Spirit Himself beareth witness with our spirit, that we are the children of God" (Rom. 8:16). Hallelujah for the assurance the Spirit brings to our hearts! But He does more:

In Ephesians 4:30 we read, ". . . Grieve not the Holy Spirit of God, *whereby ye are sealed* unto the day of redemption." And in Ephesians 1:13, 14 Paul tells us, "In whom (Christ) ye also trusted, after that ye heard the Word of truth, the Gospel of your salvation: in whom also after that ye believed, ye were *sealed with that Holy Spirit of promise, which is the earnest of our inheritance until the redemption of the purchased possession,* unto the praise of His glory.

To sum up the ministry of the Holy Ghost as having to do with the new birth and the life of the born again believer, we note that first of all the Holy Spirit draws us to God. When the sinner hears the Word, the Holy Spirit takes the Word and bears it home to the heart of the sinner, thus drawing him to God.

The Holy Spirit then convicts and convinces the sinner

that he is lost and needs a Saviour; and when the sinner hears the Word, is convicted of sin and *believes* the Word, then the Holy Spirit is the power that baptizes that person into the body of Christ, the true Church, which is made up of all born again people.

After we are baptized into the body of Christ, the Holy Ghost takes up His abode in our hearts—and FILLS us if we are willing to be emptied of self. Then, He leads us into the paths of right living, He teaches us of the deep things of God, and gives us perfect assurance of our salvation.

Last—but by no means least—the Holy Spirit SEALS us "until the day of redemption"—until Christ comes for His own! So far as the new birth is concerned, the Word of God and the Holy Ghost are Siamese twins; they cannot be separated. One cannot be born again apart from the Word of God, and it is just as true that there can be no new birth apart from the Holy Spirit. The Gospel is the power of God unto salvation to all who believe, and when Jesus said to Nicodemus, "Except a man be born of water and of the Spirit," He simply meant, "Except a man *hear* the Word and *receive* the Word, he cannot be born again."

Now let us turn again to the writings of Paul and hear more of what he has to say about the new birth (salvation):

"Moreover, brethren, I declare unto you the Gospel which I preached unto you, which also ye have received, and wherein ye stand; *by which also ye are saved,* if ye keep in memory what I preached unto you, unless ye have believed in vain. For I delivered unto you first of all that which I also received, how that Christ died for our sins according to the Scriptures; and that He was buried, and that He rose again the third day according to the Scriptures (I Cor. 15:1-4).

46

Paul clearly sets forth what he preached to the Corinthians. He said, 'I preached unto you the GOSPEL. You *received* the Gospel, you *stand* in the Gospel, you are *saved* by the Gospel"—and then he gives a clear, easily-understood *definition* of the Gospel: (1) The death (2) the burial (3) the resurrection of the Lord Jesus, "ACCORDING TO THE SCRIPTURES."

Paul preached the Gospel, and according to Paul, the heart of the Gospel is the death, burial, and resurrection of the Lord Jesus as laid down in the Word of God—not according to the way some theologian or some denomination sees it, but as recorded in God's precious, holy Word! I declare on the basis of God's Word that salvation from hell is by God's grace, through the shed blood of the Lord Jesus Christ—*plus exactly nothing.* There is not one solitary thing that man can do to save his soul, nor to *add to* his redemption.

Stewardship is another matter. Rewards are earned through faithful Christian service—but *the new birth is God's miracle,* and God alone can "born" the sinner into the body of Christ. Baptism, works, good living, morality, religion, denominational loyalty, church attendance—*nothing* that man can do or participate in will help to save or keep saved. *We are saved through the shed blood of Jesus Christ and kept by the power of God.* "For whatsoever is born of God overcometh the world: and this is the victory that overcometh the world, *even our faith"* (I John 5:4).

Flesh is flesh—and always will be, until we get our glorified bodies when Jesus comes in the Rapture. God Almighty gave up flesh in the Garden of Eden. He said to Adam, "Dust thou art, to dust thou shalt return"—but He provided the seed of the woman to deliver the soul. The reason so many believers have such a terrific battle within

47

themselves is that they do not recognize the fact of I Corinthians 10:12: *"Wherefore let him that thinketh he standeth take heed lest he fall."*

The only way the Christian can ever be victorious over the world, the flesh, and the devil is to depend wholly upon the Holy Spirit within: "Ye are of God, little children, and have overcome them: because greater is He that is in you, than he that is in the world" (I John 4:4). We *should be* victorious—and we CAN be if we will trust and obey; but as long as we live in this life we will be wrapped in a body of flesh, a body capable of committing sin, a body capable of stumbling, a body that is weak and unworthy. But we who are born again have within our bosom the divine nature of God (the Holy Spirit) to lead us into paths of right living.

We overcome because JESUS overcame. In Him, by Him, and through Him we can conquer; but without Him it is impossible to live a victorious life. The person who reaches the place where he thinks he is strong enough to overcome the devil, is in for a terrible defeat!

If you are one of those who are up today and down to-morrow, shouting the praises of God today but discouraged and in despair tomorrow, I wish you would write for my book on *The Two Natures*. Send fifty cents to the Gospel Hour, and ask for this little 32-page booklet. You will find in it a world of information and help concerning the flesh and the spirit.

A *sinner* has only ONE nature—the ungodly, sinful, nature—but the moment he puts his trust in the Lord Jesus and is born again, the divine nature of GOD comes into his heart. Paul recognized the fact that man, even though he may be a child of God, is still in the body, and he begs us to present our bodies a living sacrifice, which he says is our

48

"reasonable service" (Rom. 12:1). He prayed that the Thessalonian believers would be sanctified—soul, spirit, and body (I Thess. 5:23).

From I Corinthians 3:16 and 17 we know that Paul was aware that believers can defile the body: "Know ye not that ye are the temple of God, and that the Spirit of God dwelleth in you? If any man defile the temple of God, him shall God destroy; for the temple of God is holy, which temple ye are."

To the Galatians he put it this way: "For the flesh lusteth against the Spirit, and the Spirit against the flesh: and these are contrary the one to the other: so that ye cannot do the things that ye would. But if ye be led of the Spirit, ye are not under the law. Now the works of the flesh are manifest, which are these: Adultery, fornication, uncleanness, lasciviousness, idolatry, witchcraft, hatred, variance, emulations, wrath, strife, seditions, heresies, envyings, murders, drunkenness, revellings, and such like: of the which I tell you before, as I have told you in time past, that they which do such things shall not inherit the kingdom of God" (Gal. 5:17-21).

Here Paul clearly declares that there is warfare between the spirit and the flesh—they are contrary one to the other; but if we are led of the Spirit we will not fulfill the lust of the flesh. We must put no confidence in the flesh, but depend one hundred percent upon the Spirit. Every born again child of God should recognize the weakness of the flesh. We should yield our bodies as living sacrifices unto God and surrender our members as instruments of righteousness to be used of Him.

But many Christians do not understand the two natures —the physical and the spiritual; and many times they endure sad defeat because they do not recognize the battle that can—and DOES—exist between the spirit and the flesh.

Hear the words of Jesus: "That which is born of the flesh is flesh; and that which is born of the Spirit is spirit" (John 3:6). When God saves us He saves the spirit—*the inner man.* If Jesus tarries, these bodies of flesh will return to dust—and if the Rapture takes place during our lifetime, our bodies will be changed instantly—corruption will put on incorruption, mortality will put on immortality. I Corinthians 15:50 tells us that flesh and blood shall not inherit the kingdom of God. We will receive a new body when Jesus comes in the first resurrection.

But we do not wait until Jesus comes to become a new man: ". . . *If any man be in Christ, he is a new creature: old things are passed away; behold, all things are become new.*" In Colossians 1:27 Paul speaks of "Christ in you, the hope of glory." Christ in you brings salvation. Christ in you brings victory. Christ in you entitles you to a home in heaven. But *without Christ* you are hopeless, helpless, and hell-bound!

Evidently Nicodemus had some difficulty in understanding the process of the new birth, for in John 3:10 Jesus asked him, "Art thou a master of Israel, and knowest not these things?" In other words, "Nicodemus, you are a master in Israel, well versed in the religion of the Jews—and yet you do not understand these spiritual truths."

Beloved, Nicodemus is not the last person to hold a master's degree in religion without understanding the spiritual truth of the new birth! There are men today in the pulpits of America who have degrees from outstanding schools of theology—and yet they cannot tell their parishioners the simplicity of the new birth because they have never experienced it themselves.

Lest someone accuse me of judging, let me assure you that when a person denies the blood atonement, the virgin birth, the fact of the NEW birth—or any ONE of the fundamentals of the faith, *that person is not born again.* When we believe on the Lord Jesus Christ unto salvation we believe everything this Bible teaches concerning Christ —and if Jesus Christ were not virgin-born then His blood has no more power than the blood of any other person who died a martyr's death in the interest of religion! Jesus did not die a martyr's death. He laid His life down and shed His blood on the cross that we might be saved from everlasting damnation.

Nicodemus had a master's degree in Judaism, but he did not understand the new birth. Jesus referred to the Old Testament as He explained, "As Moses lifted up the serpent in the wilderness, even so must the Son of man be lifted up; that whosoever believeth in Him should not perish, but have eternal life" (John 3:14, 15).

Beloved, consider this: *If JESUS used the Word of God in leading Nicodemus into the light of salvation, how much MORE do ministers today need to fill their sermons with "Thus saith the Lord!"* Many sermons today contain no Scripture at all; others contain very little. I shall never understand WHY a man will bear the name of minister, stand behind the sacred desk and yet refuse to incorporate the Word of God into his message—but this is going on all over the country. Any preacher who fails to tell his people that they must be born again, will give an account at the judgment bar of God and will spend eternity in hell for leading people astray. The devil does not care how long nor how loud a man preaches, if he will just detour around the

51

Word of God with its Gospel message of the blood of Jesus.

Nicodemus was undoubtedly familiar with the account of Moses and the fiery serpents. I do not doubt that he knew that it was not the pole or the serpent of brass that saved the people, but their faith and obedience in believing and obeying God's message through Moses.

Personally, I believe Nicodemus was saved that night. If he was not born again at that time, certainly the seed was sown that later brought the light of salvation; and when the rulers of the Jews were criticizing and condemning Jesus, Nicodemus came to the defense of the Saviour (John 7:50, 51). When Jesus was crucified, Nicodemus was one of the two who came forward and claimed His body for burial (John 19:38-40).

Yes, I believe Nicodemus was born again, and I expect to meet him in the City of God. What was it that brought salvation to his heart? It was THE WORD OF GOD. When Jesus gave Nicodemus the account of Moses and the serpent, *he believed and received the Son of man even as lifted up already.*

Friend, if you are not saved, it matters not how vile or ungodly you may be—(nor how morally straight and upright you may be)—if you will bow your head this moment, believe on the Lord Jesus Christ, accept His death, burial, and resurrection by faith and put your trust in His finished work, He will save your soul. In your own way ask Jesus to come into your heart this moment. He will come in—and He will give you "joy unspeakable and full of glory."

John 3:16 (often referred to as "the Gospel in a nutshell") is probably the most beloved verse in all of the Bible. *Love* is its central theme, and as we analyze this verse

52

I pray that someone may be brought into a saving knowledge of the Lord Jesus Christ.

Love is proved by action. It makes no difference how often a man may tell his wife he loves her—if he never expresses his love through action she will find it hard to believe his words. It matters not how much our children may express their love for us in words—if they do not demonstrate that love in obedience and respect we could well *doubt* their words. God not only SAID He loved us—He PROVED it:

1. *God's love is expressive in its action:*

The height, the depth, the length and the breadth of God's love are suggested in the opening words of John 3:16 —"For God SO loved . . ." The *height* of God's love is its source. The *depth* of His love for man's necessity is suggested in the conjunction "for," connecting John 3:16 with the the two preceding verses. The *breadth* of God's love is discovered in the word "so"—*God SO loved*. And the length of God's love is made known in the word "love"—for who could measure the length of Him who IS love itself?(I John 4:8).

2. *God's love is extraordinary in its choice:*

There is nothing ordinary about God, and His love is MOST extraordinary. The marvel is that God should—or could—love the world, whose mind is enmity against Him and whose course is evil throughout. The world is selfish and self-pleasing, the heart of the world is desperately wicked, and the trend of the world is sin-ward, certainly not God-ward. The will of the world is perverse, and the god of the world is none other than the devil himself! Yet, in spite of it all, God SO LOVED the world.

Have you ever asked yourself the question, "How many

folks do I *really* love?" You may say, "O, Brother Greene— *I love everybody!*" *Do* you? How many people do you love enough *to let your child DIE for them?* Think it over. Yes, God's love is extraordinary in its choice.

3. *God's love is expensive in its sacrifice:*

He gave His only begotten Son! *Abraham* paid tithes to *Melchisedec* (Heb. 7:4-10). "Jewels of silver, and jewels of gold, and raiment" were given to *Rebekah,* Isaac's bride (Gen. 24:53). *Joseph* gave *his brethren* gifts in the land of Egypt (Gen. 45:16-23). *Caleb* gave *Achsah* the upper and nether springs (Judges 1:15). *Boaz* gave *Ruth* six measures of barley (Ruth 3:15). Because of his love for *David, Jonathan* gave up his right to the throne—but what are these gifts when compared with God's gift of His only begotten Son?

Compared with the gift of God, material gifts fade like the stars at sunrise. Think *for whom* Christ was given. Think *to what* Christ was given—and then estimate the cost of the sacrifice of Gethsemane's terrible agony! Think of the shame and the suffering of His cross. Think of the moment when heaven turned "black as sackcloth of hair," when the earth groaned in convulsions and Jesus cried out, "My God! My God! *Why hast thou forsaken me?*" I think you will agree that God's love is expensive in its sacrifice.

4. *God's love is extensive in its offer:*

The love of God offers salvation to "whosoever will." Love's eyes look upon the need of ALL—not just a select few. Love's invitation is to ALL: "Come unto me, and I will give you rest." All who come may drink freely of the water of life. Love's heart of compassion beats tenderly for all; love's feet run to meet all returning prodigals. Love's ears are open to hear all who call upon Jesus: *"Whosoever shall call upon the Name of the Lord shall be saved."* Love's will is to bless all. Love is not willing that any should perish, but that ALL come to repentance. Yes, God's love is extensive in its offer.

5. *God's love is exclusive in its bestowal:*

". . . Whosoever *believeth* on Him . . ." Belief is faith, faith is belief—the two cannot be separated. Faith is the eye which looks to Jesus and obtains life from Him. Faith is the hand which receives God's gift of His only begotten Son. Faith is the ear which hears the call of Jesus, and obeys His voice. Faith is the feet that run to Jesus at His invitation, and follow in His steps. Faith is the will that responds to God's word of direction. The Holy Spirit is the giver of faith, through the Word of God. The pure, unadulterated Word of the living God is the *ground* of faith, and the *object* of faith is the living Christ who is alive forevermore. The *outcome* of faith is a holy life. The *end* of faith is salvation. The *nature* of faith is complete trust. The *companion* of faith is love, and God's eternal blessings are only promised to faith—His love *is* exclusive in its bestowal.

6. *God's love is exceptional in its work:*

That they who believe on Christ *"should not PERISH"* expresses the exceptional, unique work of God's love. In the word "perish" we hear the groans of the damned. We feel the depth of misery, the eternal despair of the lost, the outer darkness of the pit in which are all the unsaved who have died. We feel the doom of the wicked, the failure of the sinner, the very nature of hell itself! But when man believes on Christ, God's love saves him from this terrible doom. I think you will agree that God's love IS exceptional in its work.

7. *God's love is eternal in its blessing:*

Everlasting life! Eternal life! What does it mean to possess eternal life? It means to possess HIM (I John 5:12) ;

55

and to possess Him means that we are saved with an eternal salvation, comforted with eternal consolation, liberated by eternal redemption through His blood and kept for an eternal inheritance. We are secured in an eternal covenant made by God. In Christ we are possessed by the eternal Spirit—the third Person of the Godhead; and in Christ we are loved with eternal love. Thank God for GOD!

The Psalmist describes God in these tremendous words: "Lord, thou hast been our dwelling place in all generations. Before the mountains were brought forth, or ever thou hadst formed the earth and the world, even *from everlasting to everlasting, thou art God"* (Psalm 90:1).

Yes, God's love is expressive in its action, extraordinary in its choice, expensive in its sacrifice, extensive in its offer, exclusive in its bestowal, exceptional in its work, and eternal in its blessing. Do YOU know the love of God? Have you received the Son of His love? God so loved the world that He gave His only begotten Son, that YOU, believing in Him, should not perish, but have eternal life!

"For God sent not His son into the world to condemn the world; but that the world through Him might be saved. *He that believeth on Him is NOT condemned; but he that believeth not is condemned ALREADY, because he hath not believed in the name of the only begotten Son of God"* (John 3:17, 18).

John 3:18, just quoted, presents the truth of the new birth in a threefold way:

1. It tells us who is NOT condemned.

2. It tells us of those who ARE condemned.

3. It tells us WHY they are condemned.

"He that believeth on Him is NOT condemned." To believe on Jesus is to place complete trust in Him, relying

wholeheartedly and entirely upon Him. As you would drive your automobile on a bridge that spans a river, you place your trust, your very life, on Jesus—and He will save your soul. You would not drive your automobile onto a bridge if you did not have faith in that bridge to sustain the weight of your car. To believe in Jesus completely, you must believe that He is able to save you. Do you believe that Jesus died, was buried, and rose again? Do you believe that He died to save sinners? Do you believe that He is able to save to the uttermost all who will come unto God by Him? If you believe that, then rest your case in His hands. He will save your soul, and will remove all condemnation from you. BUT—

"He that believeth NOT is condemned ALREADY." The Scripture does not say those who "believe not" are *going to be* condemned, or that they *might be* condemned. It says they are condemned *already.* All unbelievers are under the condemnation of Almighty God this very moment. It matters not how morally good they may be, if they do not believe on Jesus they are condemned NOW. One heartbeat is the only thing standing between the sinner and hell.

In the last part of this verse we find the truth as to WHY condemnation rests upon all unbelievers. *"Because he HATH NOT BELIEVED in the name of the only begotten Son of God."* In Acts 4:12 we read, "Neither is there salvation in any other: for there is none other name under heaven given among men, whereby we must be saved." Salvation is found only in Jesus. Man must believe on Him, or die in sin. If you are not a believer, the condemnation of Almighty God rests upon you NOW—and the reason God's judgment and condemnation hang heavy over your head is simply because you refuse to believe on the name of the Lord Jesus Christ.

CHAPTER III

The Simplicity of Salvation

Salvation is so simple that a child can understand it. Salvation is so free that a pauper in rags may receive it simply for the asking.

"Believe on the Lord Jesus Christ, and thou shalt be saved . . ." (Acts 16:31).

". . . As many as received Him, to them gave He power to become the sons of God, even to them that believe on His name: which were born, not of blood, nor of the will of the flesh, nor of the will of man, *but of God*" (John 1:12, 13).

God does the "borning" when the sinner does the *believing*. God does the saving when the sinner does the *receving*. ". . . Behold, NOW is the accepted time; behold, NOW is the day of salvation" (II Cor. 6:2)—and for YOU, sinner friend, five minutes from now may be too late!

By way of brief review of our study thus far in John's Gospel I would first point out that the account of Nicodemus and his coming to Jesus by night is recorded only by John. Matthew, Mark, and Luke do not mention this meeting between Jesus and Nicodemus. John tells us the *imperative* of salvation, he tells us *how* we are born again, and gives the teaching of Jesus concerning the new birth.

Nicodemus was a respectable man. He was religious, he was educated, and he was an honest seeker of truth. He was not a hypocrite, nor was he a religious fanatic. He came to Jesus with a hungry heart, he approached the Lord in the right spirit, he listened with an honest heart, and he asked sensible questions. Jesus, knowing that Nicodemus had an honest, sincere heart, answered his questions and led him step by step into the door of salvation.

We also noticed that the truth of the new birth has to do with the spirit, not with the flesh. It is a spiritual birth, of God and not of man. Not one time did Jesus suggest that Nicodemus must live a good life, unite with a church, or be immersed in water. He did not discuss works, He did not mention moral living. He simply said, "Except a man be born of water and of the Spirit, he cannot enter the kingdom of God."

But today, man has added rituals, good works, dogmas, doctrines, and creeds. Jesus preached to Nicodemus, "Ye must be born again"—and He left no loopholes. He also left no doubt in the mind of Nicodemus that the new birth has nothing to do with the flesh, but with the spirit—the part of man that will never die.

Beloved, if it were necessary to be baptized in order to be saved; if it were necessary to keep rules and regulations, obey doctrines and dogmas of modern denominations, in order to be saved, then why did not the Master Teacher tell Nicodemus that he must do these things?

I repeat—I believe a born again child of God should be baptized. I believe a born again child of God should join a local church. I believe a born again child of God should give at least ten percent of his income to the ministry of the Gospel—and I believe that a born again child of God should —and *will*—live a clean life and go about doing good. But these things are the FRUITS of salvation, they have to do with stewardship AFTER we are born again, they are not concerned with the new birth itself. Salvation is of the Lord, it comes from God. The new birth is through the *power* of God, and nothing man can do has anything to do with being born again. The new birth is entirely of the Lord—by grace, through faith, *plus nothing*.

I would remind you that Jesus used the Word of God to

lead Nicodemus into salvation. He gave him the account of Moses and the brazen serpent in the wilderness. God said to Moses, "Tell the people to look, and LIVE!" To His ministers today He is saying, "Tell sinners to believe on the Lord Jesus Christ—and live eternally!"

Beloved, by the grace of God and regardless of what man may do or say, I will preach salvation by grace until God calls me home! I refuse to add to or take from the plan of salvation—God's gift to a hell-deserving sinner. All anyone need do to come into possesson of a gift is to receive it from the giver. God so loved the world that He gave His only begotten Son, and those who *receive* His Son will be set free from sin, saved, and made ready for heaven.

In the last verse of John, chapter 3, we read, *"He that believeth on the Son hath everlasting life: and he that believeth not the Son shall not see life; but the wrath of God abideth on him."* Please notice the word "HATH"—present tense. Believers HAVE everlasting life NOW. By contrast, "He that believeth not the Son of God hath not life, but *the wrath of God ABIDETH* (present tense) *on him."* If you have not believed on the Lord Jesus Christ for salvation, the wrath of God hangs heavy over your head right NOW. May God grant that before you read another page, sinner friend, you bow your head, open your heart to Jesus, and receive Him as Saviour now. He will save you this very moment.

The fourth chapter of the Gospel of John records a very interesting interview between Jesus and the woman of Samaria. As Jesus traveled from Judaea into Galilee, "He must needs go through Samaria." Being wearied from His journey, He stopped to rest at Jacob's well. The Scripture tells us that this took place at "about the sixth hour," which would be twelve o'clock noon as we count time today.

As Jesus rested at Jacob's well, a woman of Samaria came to draw water. Please notice that Jesus opened the conversation with this woman—He did not wait for her to speak first. Christians would do well to learn a lesson from the Lord Jesus. When we go into a home or place of business, or when we meet with strangers in our daily life, if we would open the conversation in wholesome Christian language many times we would avoid being embarrassed by the *wrong* kind of language.

Jesus said to the woman, "Give me to drink." She did not quite understand this. She replied, "How is is that thou, being a Jew, askest drink of me, which am a woman of Samaria? for the Jews have no dealings with the Samaritans." Her statement was true. Bible antiquity tells us that the Jews prayed in the morning that God would deliver them from even seeing a Samaritan that day! But this Jew was asking a Samaritan woman for a drink, and she plainly showed her surprise.

Jesus answered her question by saying, "If thou knewest the gift of God, and who it is that saith to thee, Give me to drink, thou wouldest have asked of Him, and He would have given thee living water." In other words, what Jesus really said to the woman was this: "If you knew who I am and why I am passing through Samaria, you would have opened the conversation yourself. If you had recognized me, you would asked ME for a drink, and I would have given you *living water.*"

Still lacking in understanding, the woman said to Him, "Sir, thou hast nothing to draw with, and the well is deep. From whence then hast thou that living water? Art thou greater than our father Jacob, which gave us the well, and drank thereof himself?"

Like Nicodemus, she was thinking in terms of flesh, and

water that satisfies the *thirst* of the flesh. She did not think in the realm of the Spirit because she was in total ignorance concerning spiritual matters. Jesus told her that whosoever drank of the water from the well would thirst again, *"But whosoever drinketh of the water that I shall give him shall never thirst; but the water that I shall give him shall be in him a well of water springing up into everlasting life."*

Of course, this statement created a deep curiosity in the woman's heart. She had never heard of "living water" that would forever quench thirst. So she said to Him, "Sir, give me this water, that I thirst not, neither come hither to draw!" Please notice how Jesus led this woman, step by step, into the door of salvation—and remember, Jesus IS the Door; He IS salvation.

When the woman asked for the living water, Jesus said to her, "Go, call thy husband, and come hither." He knew her besetting sin, just as He knows YOUR besetting sin. If you are not born again, Jesus knows what it is that you love more and desire more than you desire to be saved. He knew this Samaritan woman was a heart-breaking harlot, and so He said to her, "Go call your husband."

She made no effort to deny the truth. She said, "I *have* no husband." Jesus commended her for telling the truth. He said, "Thou hast well said, I have no husband: For thou hast had *five* husbands and he whom thou now hast is *not* thy husband. In that saidst thou truly."

Jesus honors truth. You cannot hide your sin from Him. God knows your every thought and the intent of your heart. The Samaritan woman had not yet realized that she was talking with the Son of God, but she knew that she was speaking to a very unusual person.

Now notice how the devil immediately goes into operation and attempts to get the woman's mind off of spiritual matters. In verse 19 the woman said to Jesus, "Sir, I perceive that thou art a prophet. Our fathers worshipped in this mountain; and ye say, that in Jerusalem is the place where men ought to worship." Do you see how the devil is trying to sidetrack this conversation from living water to church membership or religious activity? This woman was not ready to worship *anywhere*—she was a poor, sinful, harlot with five living husbands and was then living with a man to whom she was not married! Yet Satan prompted her to change the conversation from salvation to religious discussion.

But Jesus immediately thwarted the devil's interference: "Jesus saith unto her, Woman . . . ye worship ye know not what! *We know* what *we* worship: for salvation is of the Jews." What He said to her, in essence, was: "Lady, you do not *need* to know *where* to worship. You are not *ready* to worship. You do not know what you are talking about. You are in total *spiritual ignorance.*"

In verses 23 and 24 of this chapter we read, ". . . The hour cometh, and now is, when the true worshippers shall worship the Father in spirit and in truth: for the Father seeketh such to worship Him. God is a Spirit: and they that worship Him must worship Him in spirit and in truth." Beloved, God is not worshipped in mountains nor in buildings—He is worshipped in the heart, in spirit and in truth. A church may be beautiful, it may be a place where people meet in the name of religion; but that does not make it a house of worship! It may be that God receives no worship from those who meet there—while on the other hand, in a cabin in the mountains, or far away on the mission field, or perhaps in a simple little country church, some precious believer worships God in spirit and in truth—from the heart. God is not necessarily found in buildings designated as places of worship; He abides in the bosom of every born again child of His. He is worshipped from the heart—yea, we have His promise that *"where two or three are gathered together in my name, there am I in the midst of them."*

The Samaritan woman then replied, "I know that Messias cometh, which is called Christ: When He is come, He will tell us all things." Jesus recognized that this dear woman was now ready for the drink of living water which she had previously requested. He had led her step by step to the Fountain of Life.

Someone—perhaps a godly mother, or grandmother, perhaps a friend—had told her of the Christ, the coming Messiah, and she remembered that *He* would be omnipotent, omniscient, and omnipresent. When she confessed this, Jesus knew that she was ready to drink of the water of life, and He simply said, "I THAT SPEAK UNTO THEE AM HE!"

Jesus spoke but seven words to this woman, but those seven words worked a miracle in her heart. She was completely changed, she became a new creature. She left her waterpot, "and went her way into the city, and saith to the men, Come, see a man, which told me all things that ever I did! *Is not this the Christ?"* In other words, she knew that no one but the Lord Jesus Christ could have told her everything she had ever done, and she was actually announcing to the men that she had met the Christ!

Beloved, what WAS it that caused her to throw away her waterpot, turn her back on the old life, run into the city and testify that she had met the most unusual Person she had ever met, and she wanted the men to meet Him? What was it that brought this tremendous miracle to the heart of the poor, sinful, Samaritan woman? What was it

65

that gave her such tremendous testimony that many of the Samaritans went to hear Jesus and were saved? The answer is found in verse 26—seven words that fell from the lips of the Son of God. These seven words dynamited the devil out of her life and opened an artesian well of living water in her soul. She was born of the water and of the Spirit. She accepted the Word, she believed the God whom Jesus declared to her, she accepted His Christ. Jesus, the Word in flesh, used the Word to lead a poor, fallen woman into the door of salvation.

Let us briefly consider some of the outstanding characteristics of God's love as clearly shown in the passage we have just covered:

1. *The love of God knows no racial barriers:*

Jesus came into the world to seek and to save that which was lost. He came to be the propitiation for ours sins—and for the sins of the whole world. He, being a Jew, loved a poor Samaritan, and saved her. He came that *"whosoever"* might be saved.

2. *The love of God knows no human limitation:*

The woman did not understand how Jesus could get water from the well when He had no visible means with which to *draw* the water. She wondered if He were greater than Jacob, who had given them the well. She did not understand that the love of God knows no human limitations. He can draw water from the well of everlasting life!

3. *The love of God knows every secret of the soul:*

Nothing can be hidden from the loving but all-seeing eyes of the Lamb of God. He told the Samaritan woman everything she had ever done—and kind reader, He knows everything YOU have ever done, everywhere you have ever gone, every thought you have ever had. His love knows no limitation when it comes to knowing every secret of every soul on earth.

4. *The love of God refuses to be sidetracked:*

The never-dying soul of the Samaritan woman was thirsty for living water—yet Satan tried to get her to change the subject, and discuss religion rather than salvation. But Jesus refused to be sidetracked. He drove home the fact that God is worshipped only in spirit and in truth. He continued speaking with the woman until she asked for the living water, and confessed, "I know Messiah cometh."

Beloved, we will never know this side of heaven the power of God's Word! No wonder the devil hates the Word of God. No wonder the modern "revisers" are trying to discredit, defeat, and tear down the fundamentals of the Christian faith! No wonder the ministers of Satan deny the Bible teaching of the virgin birth, the blood of Jesus, and the cardinal truths of old-time religion!

Oh, yes—the devil would like to trim the Word of God, modernize it, and make it sound like all other books, because he knows that the Word of God spells His defeat! He knows that sinners are saved by believing the Word of God, and therefore he is attacking the very foundation of Christianity. *If Satan could discredit the Word of God, he could wreck the faith that saves*—but thank God, he cannot undermine the Rock of Ages, the Chief Cornerstone, the Word of the living God! God's Word is forever settled in heaven —it is finished, and forever filed in safe keeping in God's Celestial City.

John 4:46-54 gives us another beautiful picture of salvation: We are told that a certain nobleman at Capernaum, whose son was sick unto death, came to Jesus and "besought Him that He would come down, and heal his son . . ."

But Jesus, knowing the hearts of all men, knew the heart of this nobleman, and He said to him, *"Except ye see signs and wonders, ye will not believe."* Undoubtedly the nobleman had heard reports of the mighty miracles of healing that Jesus had performed throughout the countryside, and he expected a spectacular miracle in the case of his sick boy. Jesus knew this, and therefore he said to the nobleman, "Unless you see some outstanding, miraculous performance, you will not believe·"

But I believe that something in the face of the Saviour, perhaps something in His voice, melted the nobleman's heart, and he then said to Jesus, "Sir, come down ere my child die." This man recognized the fact that unless Jesus healed his son, the boy was as good as dead. Christ was his only hope—and beloved, if you want God to work the miracle of salvation in your heart, YOU, too, must come to the place where you believe and confess that the only hope for you lies in the finished work of the Lord Jesus Christ. The nobleman confessed that Jesus was his only hope, and when he demonstrated such faith the Lord said to him, "Go thy way—thy son liveth." The Scripture tells us that "the man believed the word that Jesus had spoken unto him, and he went his way."

Please notice—the *nobleman "BELIEVED THE WORD that Jesus had spoken unto him."* When we believe the Word, the Word brings faith, faith brings salvation, and *every need* is supplied by faith.

Notice also that Jesus spoke the last words in the conversation between Himself and the nobleman. Jesus spoke the last word of salvation when He said, *"It is finished."* Nothing can be added to the finished product of Almighty God. Salvation is brought down to man by and through the Lord Jesus Christ, and there is not one thing you or I can add to it—and praise God, there is nothing we can *take away* from it! To tamper with God's salvation is to *wreck* salvation. It must be received from God on the terms of the Gospel. Jesus said to the nobleman, "Go thy way—thy son liveth." The man believed the words of Jesus, and went home.

Verse 51 of this chapter tells us that as the man was going down to his house, "his servants met him, and told him, saying, Thy son liveth." The nobleman then inquired as to the hour his son had begun to improve, and they told him, "Yesterday at the seventh hour the fever left him. *So the father knew that it was at the same hour, in the which Jesus said unto him, Thy son liveth:* and himself believed, and his whole house."

This dear nobleman believed the Word, a miracle was performed in the life of his sick child—and when the nobleman realized that the boy was healed at the very second Jesus had said, "Thy son liveth," he then believed that Jesus was everything He claimed to be—yea, very God in flesh. Beloved, it is the WORD that brings salvation.

In the fifth chapter of John's Gospel we find the story of a man who had been paralyzed for thirty-eight years (John 5:5). Jesus went up to Jerusalem to the feast of the Jews. He passed by the sheep market, near which there was a pool. Around the pool were five porches, and in these porches lay a great multitude of sick folk—the blind, the lame, the withered. They were waiting for the moving of the water in the pool. The Scripture tells us that "an angel went down at a certain season into the pool, and troubled the water; whosoever then first after the troubling of the water stepped in was made whole of whatsoever disease he had." (John 5:4).

Among this multitude of impotent folk was a man who

had had an infirmity for thirty-eight years, and when Jesus approached the porches filled with sick people He saw this man. "When Jesus saw him lie, and knew that he had been now a long time in that case, he saith unto him, *Wilt thou be made whole?* The impotent man answered Him, *Sir, I have no man, when the water is troubled, to put me into the pool: but while I am coming, another steppeth down before me.*"

To me, those words are among the saddest in all of the Bible! Think of it, beloved: Here lies a man, only a stone's cast from the temple, lying near the sheep market where thousands of worshippers purchased sheep and lambs to slaughter as sacrifices at the fast—and yet those thousands of worshippers passed him by for many years. Not one had found time to help him, they were not even concerned about him!

But as he looked into the compassionate face of Jesus, he saw something he had never seen before, and as he listened to the tender words of Jesus, he recognized something and felt something he had never before heard or felt in the language of man. Jesus said to Him *"Rise, take up thy bed, and walk."* Notice—only seven words—*"AND IMMEDIATELY the man was made whole, and took up his bed, and walked!"*

Immediately—not a minute later, not five minutes later, not an hour later, not the next day—but the instant Jesus said, "Rise, take up thy bed, and walk, "the man arose, took up his bed, *and walked!* What did it? It was his faith in the words of Jesus—words that invited him to get up and walk.

If ever man had an understandable right to argue with the Lord Jesus, this man had that right. For thirty-eight years he had been a victim of paralysis, unable to walk; he might well have argued with the Lord Jesus—but he did not. At those seven powerful words, the man stood up, picked up his bed, and walked. The power of those words raised him from a bed of paralysis that had held him for thirty-eight long years.

Perhaps someone reading these lines has been bound by the *devil* for thirty-eight years, or for forty-five years, or fifty years. Or perhaps some young person, serving sin for only a short while, is already feeling the paralysis of its deadly poison. If you are bound by the paralysis of sin, *hear the words of Jesus:* "Ye shall know the truth, and the truth shall make you free . . . If the Son therefore shall make you free, ye shall be free indeed" (John 8:32, 36). Tenderly, compassionately, He invites you, "Come unto me, and I will give you rest . . . Call on me, and I will save your soul . . . Believe on me, and I will forgive your sins!"

Dear reader, if you do not know Christ as your Saviour, will you not listen to His wonderful words of life? Will you not bow your head this moment, believe on the Lord Jesus Christ, and let Him deliver you from the paralysis of sin? You CAN overcome the sin that has cast you down, sin that has bound your soul as surely as physical paralysis cripples the body. All you need do is believe the words of Jesus and ask Him to save your soul.

Thus far, we have considered Nicodemus—an educated religionist, a Pharisee, a ruler of the Jews. Jesus gave to him the wonderful words of life, he *believed* those words— and was born again (John, chapter 3).

In the fourth chapter of John's Gospel we studied the account of the Samaritan woman as Jesus gave to her the water of life. She believed His words, and the power of the Gospel changed her from a heart-breaking harlot into an evangelist. She came to the wall with an empty waterpot—

she ran back to town with an artesian well of living water bubbling in her soul!

In the last verses of chapter 4, we learned of the nobleman who came to Jesus on behalf of his dying boy, he believed the words of Jesus—and not only was his son healed, but a miracle was wrought in his own life and that of his household. They believed the wonderful words of life and were born again.

In John chapter 5 we read of the dear man who had been paralyzed for thirty-eight years. He was within a stone's cast of the temple in Jerusalem, yet the worshippers had passed him by. Not one of them had found time to help him. But when Jesus said, "Rise, take up thy bed and walk," he *believed* those words, and they brought healing to his paralyzed body as well as deliverance to his soul.

But in John chapter 6 we find quite a different story. When Jesus gave His discourse on the bread of life, the Jews murmured and strove among themselves as to how these things could be. He proclaimed, "I am the living bread which came down from heaven; if any man eat of this bread, he shall live for ever; and the bread that I will give is my flesh, which I will give for the life of the world . . . Verily, verily, I say unto you, Except ye eat the flesh of the Son of man, and drink His blood, ye have no life in you. Whoso eateth my flesh, and drinketh my blood, hath eternal life . . ."

The people murmured and said "This is an hard saying: who can hear it? . . . From that time many of His disciples went back, and walked no more with Him" (John 6:60 and 66). They refused to believe the words of Jesus, they refused to accept the tremendous truth he had just presented.

Jesus then turned to the twelve and asked, "*Will YE*

72

ALSO *go away?"* Simon Peter answered: "Lord, to whom shall we go? *Thou hast the words of eternal life.* And we believe and are sure that thou are that Christ, the Son of the living God" (John 6:67-69).

Had the twelve desired to follow the masses and go away, they could have done so—they were men of their own free will. They were free to turn their backs on the teaching of Jesus, free to reject His words of life. But thank God for Peter's tremendous proclamation: *"THOU hast the WORDS of eternal life!"*

Eternal life comes only through the Word of God: *"In the beginning was the Word, and the Word was with God, and the Word was God"* (John 1:1).

We are saved by grace through faith: "So then faith cometh by hearing, and hearing *by the Word of God"* (Rom. 10:17).

"Verily, verily, I say unto thee, Except a man be *born again,* he cannot see the kingdom of God" (John 3:3).

". . . Being *born again,* not of corruptible seed, but of incorruptible, *by the Word of God,* which liveth and abideth for ever" (I Pet. 1:23).

Apart from the Word there is no salvation. Apart from the Word, there can be no new birth, and apart from the new birth, men are hell-bound! Believe the Word, receive the Christ—and God will "born" you into the family of heaven.

Studying still further in the Gospel of John, we find that chapter 8 presents another picture of salvation. In verses 1 and 2 of this chapter we read, "Jesus went unto the Mount of Olives. And early in the morning He came again into the temple, and all the people came unto Him; and He sat down, and taught them."

As Jesus was teaching this early morning Bible class in the temple, the Scribes and Pharisees brought a woman to Him, set her in the midst of the people and said, "Master, this woman was taken in adultery, in the very act. Now Moses in the law commanded us, that such should be stoned: *but what sayest thou?* This they said, *tempting Him,* that they might have to accuse Him."

These self-righteous Scribes and Pharisees were not really interested in getting an adulteress saved. They were not interested in cleaning up the town and ridding it of such sinful characters. *They were interested in condemning the Lord Jesus!* They wanted something whereby they could accuse Him. Instead of canvassing the city in an effort to win souls, they were very likely up before daylight searching the alleys to find a victim through which they could accuse and condemn the Saviour! So—they brought before Him a woman whom they claimed to have taken in the act of adultery; and they said to Him, "Moses said STONE HER. Now what do YOU say?"

If He said, "Let her go," He would be found guilty of breaking the law of Moses. If He said, "Stone her," He would contradict His own teaching. The Scribes and Pharisees thought they had Him in a trap from which He could not escape. "But Jesus stooped down, and with His finger wrote on the ground, as though He heard them not."

(What He wrote, the Scripture does not tell us, and there is no need to speculate. *Whatever* He wrote condemned the Scribes and Pharisees, and brought salvation to the harlot they had brought before Him.)

But they were not satisfied. They continued to ask Him: "So when they continued asking Him, He lifted up Himself, and said unto them, *He that is without sin among you,* let him first cast a stone at her."

Personally, I think Jesus knew that those men were every one guilty of committing adultery—possibly with that very woman. Knowing their hearts, He said to them, "Any one of you who is without sin, YOU cast the first stone." Again He stooped down and wrote on the ground— and again the Scripture does not tell us what He wrote; but whatever He wrote was the Word of God, because *Jesus was God in flesh.*

"And they which heard it, being convicted by their own conscience, went out one by one, beginning at the eldest, even unto the last: and Jesus was left alone, and the woman stading in the midst" (John 8:9).

Jesus stood up and looked around. He saw none but the woman, and He asked her, "Where are those thine accusers? Hath no man condemned thee?"Those must have been sweet words to the ears of that poor woman as she stood trembling, frightened half to death, expecting a deluge of stones to beat the life from her body! But instead, she heard the kind, compassionate voice of Jesus: "Where are your accusers? Has no one condemned you?" and she answered, *"No man, Lord."*

How in the world did this poor woman know that she was standing in the presence of the Lord? I believe the answer is found in I Corinthians 12:3. Paul said, "Wherefore I give you to understand, that no man speaking by the Spirit of God, calleth Jesus accursed: and that *no man can say that Jesus is the Lord, but by the Holy Ghost."* The woman watched Jesus as He wrote on the ground. Whatever He wrote convicted her of sin, convinced her that she needed a Saviour, and the words that He wrote brought saving faith to her soul. She knew that none save the Lord God Almighty could write such words, and she had heard Jesus invite any of those men who were without sin, to cast a stone at her. Therefore, she knew that He had, in so many words, told them what they had been doing. She recognized Him as the Lord of heaven, she addressed Him as Lord— and the Bible says that *"whosoever shall call upon the name of the Lord shall be saved."*

I John 5:1 tells us that "whosoever believeth that Jesus is the Christ is born of God." The woman *believed* that Jesus was the Lord, she *confessed* that He was Lord—and then those unbelievably kind words as He lifted condemnation from her soul: *"Neither do I condemn thee. Go, and sin no more!"* Hallelujah! *What a Saviour!*

The entire ninth chapter of the Gospel of John is given to the account of a young man who was born blind, and to whom Jesus gave sight—both physical and spiritual. The story presents a wonderful picture of salvation.

Seeing this young man who had been blind since birth, the disciples asked Jesus, "Master, who did sin, this man, or his parents, that he was born blind?" Jesus replied that neither this young man NOR his parents had committed the sin that brought his blindness, *". . . but that the works of God should be made manifest in him."*

Some of the dearest saints on this earth are blind people —physically blind; but blindness is not necessarily a curse —it can be a tremendous blessing, as can other physical handicaps. It is possible to glorify God in spite of sickness and physical handicaps.

As Jesus looked upon the blind young man, He said, "As long as I am in the world, *I am the light of the world.* When He had thus spoken, He spat on the ground, and made clay of the spittle, and He anointed the eyes of the blind man with the clay, and said unto him,   Go, wash in the pool of

Siloam . . . He went his way, therefore, and washed, *and came seeing!*" (John 9:5-7).

Remember—this young man could not see Jesus, and there is no record that he had ever met Him before this occasion. Perhaps he had *heard* about Him and the great miracles He had performed, but insofar as the Scripture tells us, he did not know Jesus personally. Yet—he obeyed.

The Lord did not tell this young man to go and wash in his basin at home. He did not tell him to go and wash in the river of Jordan. He gave *seven words* of specific instruction: *"Go, wash in the pool of Siloam."* The Bible tells us that the young man went his way, "and washed—AND CAME SEEING." But notice that he did not see until he obeyed the Word of God. When he followed the instructions Jesus gave him, when he went and washed in the pool designated by the Lord, his blinded eyes were immediately opened and "he came seeing."

What worked the miracle in this young man's life? *He obeyed the Word of God!* Sinner friend, if your spiritual eyes are ever opened, it will be because you hear the Word of God and obey "Thus saith the Lord!"

The neighbors of the young man were quite amazed when he received his sight. They asked him how it came about, and he replied, "A man that is called Jesus made clay, and anointed mine eyes, and said unto me, Go to the pool of Siloam, and wash: and I went and washed, and I received sight."

They then brought him to the Pharisees, who also asked him how the miracle had come about. He replied, "He put clay upon mine eyes, and I washed, and do see." The Pharisees were much disturbed, so much that they went to the boy's parents and asked them how their son had received his sight—and their reaction was, to my way of thinking, one of the tragedies recorded in the Bible. They said, "We know that this is our son, and that he was born blind: *but by what means he now seeth, we know not; or who opened his eyes, we know not:* he is of age—ask him. He shall speak for himself."

God pity the parents who would deny the truth concerning the miracle-working Son of God who opened the eyes of their boy who had never seen the light of day! It seems to me that they would have been so grateful they would have shouted the praises of Jesus from the housetops—but they did not. *For fear of the Jews* they denied any knowledge of the Saviour.

And they are not the last to deny the Lord. The reason some church members today do not sing the praises of Jesus is simply because they know they would be ostracized, pushed out, and ignored by the religious "big shots" of our day. They prefer to stand in with the denominational bosses, rather than with the Holy Spirit. They had rather be friends with the religious "powers that be" than with the Lord Jesus Christ.

The Pharisees again talked with the young man. They said, "Give GOD the praise: we know that this man (Jesus) is a sinner." The boy replied, *"Whether He be a sinner or no, I know not: ONE THING I KNOW, that, whereas I was blind, NOW I SEE!"*

Hallelujah for the boldness of this young man! He did not deny the Christ. He said, "I do not know who He is, but one thing I DO know: He and He ALONE opened my eyes, and I will not give the credit to anyone else. He is the One who opened my eyes, and to Him shall be the praise!"

Beloved, you may not be able to be a missionary, a min-

78

ister, or an evangelist, you may not be able to give hundreds of dollars to help spread the Gospel—but you can certainly raise your hand for Jesus. You can certainly speak a word of praise for all He has done for you. *Stand up for Jesus*— no matter what the cost. Stand up for Jesus, even if it costs you every friend you have. Never deny Him—because He is the only One who can keep you out of hell. If I had ten thousand hands, I would gladly raise them all for Jesus!

The Pharisees refused to accept the young man's testimony, and kept asking, "Who did it? What was His name? Who gave you your sight?" The boy finally said, "I have told you already, and ye did not hear—wherefore would ye hear it again? *Will ye also be His disciples?*" This angered the Pharisees beyond all reason, and they reviled the boy. They said, "We know that God spake unto Moses: as for this fellow, we know not from whence He is."

The next five verses are interesting indeed. The young man said to the Pharisees, "Why herein is a marvelous thing, that ye know not from whence He is, and yet He hath opened mine eyes. Now we know that God heareth not sinners: but if any man be a worshipper of God, and doeth His will, him He heareth. Since the world began was it not heard that any man opened the eyes of one that was born blind. If the man were not of God, He could do nothing.

"They answered and said unto him, Thou wast altogether born in sins, and dost thou teach us? AND THEY CAST HIM OUT."

They actually cast this boy out of the synagogue—but Jesus heard about it—and He went in search of him:

"And when He had found him, He said unto him, Dost thou believe on the Son of God? (The young man) answered and said, Who IS He, Lord, that I might believe on Him?

And Jesus said unto him, Thou hast both seen Him, and it is He that talketh with thee. And (the young man) said, *Lord, I believe.* And he worshipped Him."

Jesus found this young man after they had literally (I believe *bodily*) thrown him out of the Synagogue—and He asked the boy, "Do you believe in the Son of God?" The boy very frankly said, "I do not know who the Son of God IS, but if I DID know, I would believe on Him." Then Jesus said, "It is He that talketh with thee"—seven glorious words! But those seven words spoken by the Lamb of God transformed the life of the young man and saved his soul.

How do I know that he was saved? I know because verse 38 tells me that he *believed,* and following his believing, *he worshipped Jesus.* It all came about through the power of the words spoken to him by the Son of God. He was born again—"not of corruptible seed, but incorruptible, *by the Word of God* which liveth and abideth forever."

I would like to point out just a few verses in the remaining chapters of this marvelous Gospel of salvation:

John 10:1, 9: "Verily, verily, I say unto you, He that entereth not by the door into the sheepfold, but climbeth up some other way, the same is a thief and a robber . . . *I AM THE DOOR: by me if any man enter in, he shall be saved,* and shall go in and out and find pasture."

There is no reason for misunderstanding these words of Jesus. There is only one Door to salvation, there is only one Way to heaven—and that is through and by the Lord Jesus Christ.

The first six verses in chapter 14 are dear to my heart. Jesus had told His disciples of His coming journey to Jerusalem, of His arrest, trial, and approaching death. This saddened their hearts, and Jesus knew that they were very despondent and discouraged. Therefore, he encouraged them with these precious words:

"Let not your heart be troubled: ye believe in God, believe also in me. In my Father's house are many mansions: if it were not so, I would have told you. I go to prepare a place for you. And if I go and prepare a place for you, I will come again, and receive you unto myself; that where I am, there ye may be also. And whither I go ye know, and the way ye know.

"Thomas saith unto Him, Lord, we know not whither thou goest; and how can we know the way? Jesus saith unto him, I am the WAY, the TRUTH, and the LIFE: No man cometh unto the Father, but by me."

Thank God for Thomas! Oh, I know he has been abused and looked down upon. He has been called "Doubting Thomas," and very few have realized the import of the question he asked of Jesus, for the answer to that question gives a detailed—yet brief—account of the ONLY way to be saved. Jesus answered Thomas, *"I am the Way*—not *one* of the ways, not just *a* way—but THE way. I am the Truth —not just *part* of the truth, not *a* truth—but THE Truth. I am the Life—not just *life*, not *a* life—but THE Life."

And then He drives home the solemn fact of ONE Door, ONE Way, ONE Truth, ONE salvation: "NO MAN COMETH UNTO THE FATHER BUT BY ME!"

Beloved, this is a solemn consideration: Why did Jesus not say, "No man cometh unto the Father but by the baptistry, or by church membership, or by good works, clean living, generous giving, being sincere or being conscientiously religious"? Why did He say, "No man cometh unto the Father but BY ME"?

81

The answer is clear: According to God's Word, there IS only one way to heaven, that *one* way is by the new birth, and *the new birth comes only through and by the Lord Jesus.*

Jesus took a body, and in that body He paid sin's debt and did for man what man could never have done for himself. Jesus took upon Himself the likeness of sinful flesh, and for sin condemned sin IN the flesh, that WE, by receiving Jesus, might become the rghteousness of God—but ONLY IN CHRIST. He is the only way to heaven, and apart from Him there is no salvation.

I opened this message by asking, "Can morality save us?" The answer is clearly set forth in John's Gospel. You will notice that not once did Jesus tell anyone to clean up, change habits, or become moral. He gave them the pure, unadulterated Word. He spoke wonderful words of life to each individual. In each of the instances we have covered in this study, the words spoken by Jesus brought light, healing, understanding, redemption, and new creation to each heart.

You will note that Matthew, Mark, and Luke do not record any of the accounts which we have just studied from the Gospel of John. Why? Because John is the *salvation book.* John wrote primarily in the interest of pointing out the simplicity of the new birth. All of the Gospels are the Word of God, and each Gospel has a peculiar message of its own; but John's Gospel is distinctly the salvation book.

I praise God from the depths of my soul for the marvelous Gospel of John. In the course of my years in the ministry I have seen thousands born into the kingdom of God through these marvelous words of life: *"Ye must be born again . . . Except a man be born again he cannot see*

82

the kingdom of God . . . Except a man be born of water (the Word) *and of the Spirit, he cannot enter into the kingdom of God."*

Beloved, I have given this message on the new birth (or *"Can morality save us?"*) with love in my heart. I have not tried to defend a denomination or a religion. I have simply tried to present, in love and with a sincere heart, the precious Word of God that is able to make you wise unto salvation. If you refuse to be born again according to the terms of the Word of God, you will burn in hell—there is no alternative. You cannot enter God's celestial city unless you are born again *"according to the Scriptures":*

"Verily, verily, I say unto you, He that heareth my Word, and believeth on Him that sent me, hath everlasting life, and shall not come into condemnation: but is passed from death unto life" (John 5:24).

"Wherewithal shall a young man cleanse his way? by taking heed thereto according to thy Word" (Psalm 119:9).

"Thy Word is a lamp unto my feet, and a light unto my path" (Psalm 119:105).

"For ever, O Lord, thy Word is settled in heaven" (Psalm 119:89).

Redemption

REDEMPTION

"Blessed be the God and Father of our Lord Jesus Christ, who hath blessed us with all spiritual blessings in heavenly places in Christ: According as He hath chosen us in Him before the foundation of the world, that we should be holy and without blame before Him in love: Having predestinated us unto the adoption of children by Jesus Christ Himself, according to the good pleasure of His will, to the praise of the glory of His grace, wherein He hath made us accepted in the beloved. IN WHOM WE HAVE REDEMPTION THROUGH HIS BLOOD, THE FORGIVENESS OF SINS, ACCORDING TO THE RICHES OF HIS GRACE; wherein He hath abounded toward us in all wisdom and prudence; having made known unto us the mystery of His will, according to His good pleasure which He hath purposed in Himself: That in the dispensation of the fulness of times He might gather together in one all things in Christ, both which are in heaven, and which are on earth; even in Him: In whom also we have obtained an inheritance, being predestinated according to the purpose of Him who worketh all things after the counsel of His own will: That we should be to the praise of His glory, who first trusted in Christ. In whom ye also trusted, after that ye heard the word of truth, the Gospel of your salvation: in whom after that ye believed, ye were sealed with that holy Spirit of promise, which is the earnest of our inheritance until the redemption of the purchased possession, unto the praise of His glory" (Eph. 1:3-14).

In Genesis 3:15 God promised the seed of the woman that would crush the seed of the serpent. In Galatians 4:4 Paul tells us that in the fulness of the time, the seed of the woman came exactly as prophesied, ". . . made of a woman, made under the law, *to redeem them that were under the law,* that we might receive the adoption of sons."

The Greek word *exagorazo* denotes "to buy out" — especially in purchasing a slave with a view to his freedom. The word is used metaphorically in Galatians 3:13 and 4:5 concerning Christ's deliverance of Christian Jews from the law and its curse. However, the Greek word in our text is a noun — *apolutrosis* (a strengthened form of *exagorazo*) and is used as of *a deliverance from physical torture* (Heb. 11:35). It is also used in connection with the deliverance of the people of God at the second coming of Christ in the revelation when He comes with His glorified saints, and having to do with a redemption to be accomplished at His coming: "And then shall they see the Son of man coming in a cloud with power and great glory" (Luke 21:27).

Apolutrosis, the Greek noun used for redemption in our test, denotes forgiveness, justification, redemption as the result of expiation, and deliverance from the guilt of sins through the redemption that is in Christ Jesus (Eph. 1:7). The same word in Colossians 1:14 is translated *"the forgiveness of sins,"* which indicates both liberation from the guilt and doom of sin, and also the introduction into a life of liberty, defined as "newness of life" (Rom. 6:4).

In Hebrews 9:15 we read,". . .for the redemption of the transgressions that were under the first testament . . ." Here, *redemption OF* is equivalent to *redemption FROM,* used in the Greek in the genitive case, being used of *the object* from which *the redemption* is effective — not from the *consequence* of the transgressions, but from the transgressions themselves. The deliverance of the believer from the presence and power of sin and the deliverance of his body from bondage to corruption will occur at the coming of the Lord Jesus Christ. Study I Thessalonians 4:13-18; Romans 8:23; I Corinthians 1:30; and Ephesians 1:14; 4:30.

THE *WHEN* OF REDEMPTION

"In whom we have redemption through His blood, the forgiveness of sins, according to the riches of His grace."

Redemption is ours *NOW*. We do not pray, "Lord, *at last* redeem us in heaven," or, "Save us at the end of life's journey." *We are redeemed here and now!* It is the spiritual birthright of every believer to have the blessed assurance that redemption from sin is a personal, present possession. It is not to be ours at some future date or when we are finally inside the Pearly Gates, but redemption is ours NOW because Jesus paid in full the price sin demanded. Therefore, God can be just and yet justify the ungodly when the ungodly exercise faith in the Redeemer. Jesus redeemed (bought back) on Calvary all that Adam lost in the Garden of Eden.

The redemption Jesus purchased for us is a present possession — and it is also eternal: "But Christ being come as high priest of good things to come, by a greater and more perfect tabernacle, not made with hands, that is to say, not of this building; neither by the blood of goats and calves, but by His own blood He entered in once into the holy place, having obtained eternal redemption for us. For if the blood of bulls and of goats, and the ashes of an heifer sprinkling the unclean, sanctifieth to the purifying of the flesh: how much more shall the blood of Christ, who through the eternal Spirit offered Himself without spot to God, purge your conscience from dead works to serve the living God?" (Heb. 9:11-14).

What a marvelous fact — divinely stated by the eternal Spirit and penned down by the apostle Paul — a statement made possible through the blood of Jesus, a truth given to us by our God who cannot lie (Tit. 1:2; Heb. 6:18).

THE *HOW* OF REDEMPTION

There are many religions, many cults, and many and varied ideas concerning the interpretation of the Bible. Some maintain that every man has a right to his own religion. It is true that every individual is a free moral agent, and it is by his own free will that man must choose his way of life and where he will spend eternity. God is not a dictator, He does not force salvation upon anyone. Every man is free to set up his own religion — but in so doing, he must then write his own Bible; and if he desires to follow his own way then he must also build a heaven for himself, because the holy Word of God declares, "... *I (Jesus) am the Way, the Truth, and the Life: No man cometh unto the Father, but by me!"* (John 14:6).

"IN WHOM we have redemption . . ." The *"whom"* is Jesus. He alone satisfied the heart of God, the law of God, and all the demands of the righteousness and purity of Almighty God. In I Corinthians 1:26-31 Paul said:

"For ye see your calling, brethren, how that not many wise men after the flesh, not many mighty, not many noble, are called: But God hath chosen the foolish things of the world to confound the wise; and God hath chosen the weak things of the world to confound the things which are mighty; and base things of the world, and things which are despised, hath God chosen, yea, and things which are not, to bring to nought things that are: *That no flesh should glory in His presence. But of Him are ye in Christ Jesus, who of God is made unto us wisdom, and righteousness, and sanctification, and redemption: That, according as it is written, HE THAT GLORIETH, LET HIM GLORY IN THE LORD!"*

God has seen to it that flesh will never glory in His presence. He gave up flesh in the Garden of Eden. To Adam He said, "Dust thou art. To dust thou shalt return." (He was speaking of the body, not of the spirit.) God promised a Deliverer for the spirit but He made no provision for the flesh. When Jesus came into the world, God gave Him a body like unto sinful man, and in that body Jesus did what flesh had never done nor ever could do. When He comes in the Rapture, we will receive a glorified body like unto His resurrection body.

". . . Of Him are ye in Christ Jesus . . ." The only possible way any poor, hell-deserving sinner can please God is in the Son of God's love. Of Jesus, the Father said, "This is my beloved Son, in whom I am well pleased" (Matt. 3:17). Again, "This is my beloved Son, in whom I am well pleased; hear ye Him" (Matt. 17:5). God is highly pleased with Jesus. The Son came into the world to do the will of the Father, and every step He took, every word He spoke, every miracle He performed was to glorify the heavenly Father.

When He came to the end of His earthly ministry He turned His eyes toward God's house and said, "Father, the hour is come; glorify thy Son, that thy Son also may glorify thee: As thou hast given Him power over all flesh, that He should give eternal life to as many as thou hast given Him. And this is life eternal, that they might know thee the only true God, and Jesus Christ, whom thou hast sent. *I have glorified thee on the earth: I have finished the work which thou gavest me to do. And now, O Father, glorify thou me with thine own self with the glory which I had with thee before the world was"* (John 17:1-5).

On another occasion, when Jesus saw the exceeding sinfulness of sin, and the exceeding bitterness of the cup that He must drink, He said, "Now is my soul troubled; and what shall I say? Father, save me from this hour: but for this cause came I unto this hour. Father, glorify thy name. *Then came there a voice from heaven, saying, I have both glorified it, and will glorify it again.* The people therefore, that stood by, and heard it, said that it thundered: others said, An angel spake to Him" (John 12:27-29). Please note: Some people thought it thundered, others thought an angel spoke — but it was God the Father answering God the Son who had come into this world to purchase salvation at the tremendous price of His own precious blood.

Redemption is not in church membership, nor in the baptistry, nor in receiving communion. Redemption is not found in living a good life. Redemption is "IN WHOM" . . . *in Jesus.*

Only the grace of God brings salvation, and "the grace of God that bringeth salvation hath appeared to all men, *teaching us that, denying ungodliness and worldly lusts, we should live soberly, righteously, and godly, in this present world; LOOKING FOR THAT BLESSED HOPE, AND THE GLORIOUS APPEARING OF THE GREAT GOD AND OUR SAVIOUR JESUS CHRIST;* Who gave Himself for us, that He might redeem us from ALL iniquity, and purify unto Himself a peculiar people, zealous of good works" (Titus 2:11-14).

The grace of God that brings salvation also teaches us to deny ungodliness and to live sober, righteous lives in this present world as we look for "the glorious appearing of the great God and our Saviour Jesus Christ," who willingly gave Himself for us that He might redeem us — not partially, but *wholly* — from ALL iniquity. Redemption is IN CHRIST, and Christ alone.

REDEEMED THROUGH *WHAT?*

We have redemption now, our redemption is eternal, and our redemption is in the Lord Jesus Christ; but *through what power* are we redeemed?

"In whom we have redemption THROUGH HIS BLOOD . . ." (Eph. 1:7). The message of *the blood of Jesus* is the message most hated by the devil. The virgin birth is behind us — we KNOW that Jesus was virgin born. Calvary is behind us — we KNOW He died on the cross, His blood has been shed. Satan also knows these facts, he knows it is the precious blood of Jesus that keeps the sinner out of hell. Therefore, he cares not how long, loud, and sincerely a minister may preach — so long as he leaves out the message of the blood. He cares not how clean, upright, and conscientious a person may be in personal living, because "all of our righteousnesses are as filthy rags" (Isa. 64:6). Satan knows that we cannot earn our salvation through righteous living; he knows that only the blood brings salvation:

"Forasmuch as ye know that ye were not redeemed with corruptible things, as silver and gold, from your vain conversation received by tradition from your fathers; BUT WITH THE PRECIOUS BLOOD OF CHRIST, as of a lamb without blemish and without spot: Who verily was foreordained before the foundation of the world, but was manifest in these last times for you. Who by Him do believe in God, that raised Him up from the dead, and gave Him glory; that your faith and hope might be in God" (I Pet. 1:18-21).

93

Silver and gold cannot redeem the soul. Silver and gold cannot buy back what Adam sold to the devil in the Garden of Eden. We are redeemed only by the precious blood of Jesus — the Lamb without spot or blemish, who willingly went to the cross and carried our sins with Him there:

"Who His own self bare our sins in His own body on the tree, that we, being dead to sins, should live unto righteousness: by whose stripes ye were healed" (I Pet. 2:24).

"For what the law could not do, in that it was weak through the flesh, God sending His own Son in the likeness of sinful flesh, and for sin, condemned sin in the flesh, that the righteousness of the law might be fulfilled in us, who walk not after the flesh, but after the Spirit" (Rom. 8:3, 4).

In Hebrews 10:1-6 Paul tells us, "For the law having a shadow of good things to come, and not the very image of the things, can never with those sacrifices which they offered year by year continually make the comers thereunto perfect. For then would they not have ceased to be offered? because that the worshippers once purged should have had no more conscience of sins. But in those sacrifices there is a remembrance again made of sins every year. For it is not possible that the blood of bulls and of goats should take away sins. Wherefore when He cometh into the world, He saith, Sacrifice and offering thou wouldest not, but a body hast thou prepared me: In burnt-offerings and sacrifices for sin thou hast had no pleasure."

According to these words from the inspired pen of the Apostle Paul, who was chosen of God to make known the mystery hidden from the foundation of the world (the mystery of the grace of God), the burnt offerings and sacrifices for sins up to Calvary brought no pleasure to the great heart of God. When God looked down from Eden to Calvary and saw the animals and doves butchered and the blood offered by the high priest, it brought no pleasure to Him because it was only a shadow of things to come. Then in the fulness of time the LAMB came — the Son of God's love; but He did not come to make a sacrifice: *He WAS that sacrifice.* He came to offer Himself on the altar.

Continuing in the same chapter of Hebrews, we read: "Then said I, Lo, I come (in the volume of the book it is written of me,) to do thy will, O God. Above when He said, Sacrifice and offering and burnt-offerings and offering for sin thou wouldest not, neither hadst pleasure therein; which are offered by the law; then said He, Lo, I come to do thy will, O God. He taketh away the first, that He may establish the second. By the which will we are sanctified through the offering of the body of Jesus Christ once for all. And every priest standeth daily ministering and offering oftentimes the same sacrifices, which can never take away sins: But this man (Jesus), after He had offered one sacrifice for sins for ever, sat down on the right hand of God; from henceforth expecting till His enemies be made His footstool. *For by one offering He hath perfected for ever them that are sanctified* . . . And their sins and iniquities will I remember no more. Now where remission of these is, there is no more offering for sin. Having therefore, brethren, boldness to enter into the holiest by the blood of Jesus, by a new and living way, which He hath consecrated for us, through the veil, that is to say, His flesh" (Heb. 6:11-20 in part).

"In the volume of the book it is written . . ." The Old Testament Scriptures from Genesis through Malachi point to the Lamb without spot or blemish. Jehovah God had no pleasure in the animals slain, the blood shed, and the offer-

ings made until the Lamb, the Son of His love, laid His own life down, willingly and freely.

Unlike the offerings made by the high priest again and again, day by day and year by year, Jesus offered Himself ONCE, a sacrifice never to be repeated. And by this one offering *"perfected for ever, eternally, everlastingly,* them that are sanctified." (Christ is made unto us "wisdom, righteousness, *sanctification,* and redemption" — I Cor. 1:30.)

This is the day of liberalism and bloodless preaching; but regardless of what any minister or evangelist may say, ". . . WITHOUT SHEDDING OF BLOOD IS NO REMISSION!" (Heb. 9:22). God had His say before these self-appointed authorities on the Scriptures arrived on the scene. The Holy Spirit dictated these words to John the Beloved:

"That which was from the beginning (Jesus), which we have heard, which we have seen with our eyes, which we have looked upon, and our hands have handled, of the Word of life; (For the life was manifested, and we have seen it, and bear witness, and shew unto you that eternal life, which was with the Father, and was manifested unto us;) That which we have seen and heard declare we unto you, that ye also may have fellowship with us: and truly our fellowship is with the Father, and with His Son Jesus Christ. And these things write we unto you, that your joy may be full.

"This then is the message which we have heard of Him, and declared unto you, that God is light, and in Him is no darkness at all. If we say that we have fellowship with Him, and walk in darkness, we lie, and do not the truth: But if we walk in the light, as He is in the light, we have fellowship one with another, and the blood of Jesus Christ His Son cleanseth us from all sin" (I John 1:1-7).

Dearly beloved, the message is twofold: (1) God is light, and in Him is no darkness. (2) The blood of Jesus cleanses from all sin. There are many today who scoff at the blood, but God's Word still declares, "Without shedding of blood is no remission," and "The blood of Jesus Christ His Son cleanseth us from all sin!" Sinner friend, you will either get under the blood by faith in the finished work of Jesus Christ — or you will roast in hell forever! There is no way to eternal life save through the power of the blood of Jesus.

FROM WHAT ARE WE REDEEMED?

Jesus came into the world to seek and to save that which was lost. He came — not to be ministered unto, but to minister — and to give His life a ransom for many. He never worked a miracle to bring comfort to Himself or gain to His own pocket. He had no house to live in, no bed in which to sleep. He borrowed a boat from which He preached to the multitudes, He borrowed a little boy's lunch and fed five thousand hungry men and their families. He *"gave Himself for us, that He might redeem us from all iniquity, and purify unto Himself a peculiar people"* (Tit. 2:14).

Through the shed blood of Jesus Christ, believers are NOW (present tense) REDEEMED FROM ALL INIQUITY. The blood of Jesus covers ALL guilt, ALL iniquity— and the glorious truth is that the blood covers NOW. Through the disobedience of Adam, sin moved upon mankind, and death by sin. If you will read the first six chapters of Genesis you will see that sin brings sorrow, heartache, and destruction. Sin brought the curse: "For we know that the whole creation groaneth and travaileth in pain together until now" (Rom. 8:22). Paul tells us plainly,

97

"Wherefore as by one man sin entered into the world, and death by sin; and so death passed upon all men, for that all have sinned" (Rom. 5:12).

But the curse that came upon us because of Adam's sin can be lifted through the obedience of the second Adam — Jesus Christ: "Christ hath redeemed us from the curse of the law, being made a curse for us: for it is written, Cursed is every one that hangeth on a tree" (Gal. 3:13).

Knowing the awful ugliness of sin, the unbearable bitterness of the cup, and seeing the blackness of death, the Lord Jesus Christ fell prostrate in prayer, His perspiration stained with blood as He prayed, "Father, if thou be willing, remove this cup from me: Nevertheless *not my will, but thine, be done*" (Luke 22:42).

Jesus became a curse that WE might become the sons of God. He took the sinner's place, and suffered all the shame, all the ugliness, woe, misery, and pain that hell could heap upon the sinner. He bore it all — THAT WE MIGHT BE REDEEMED. God thundered out, "The soul that sinneth shall surely die!" and He has not changed His mind. But Jesus took the sinner's place. He died that we, through faith in His finished work, might live.

What IS sin? I John 3:4 tells us, "Whosoever committeth sin transgresseth also the law: *for sin is the transgression of the law.*" We have all sinned, we have all transgressed God's law. But Jesus fulfilled every jot and tittle of God's law: "Think not that I am come to destroy the law, or the prophets: I am not come to destroy, but to fulfill. For verily I say unto you, Till heaven and earth pass, one jot or one tittle shall in no wise pass from the law, till all be fulfilled" (Matt. 5:17, 18).

Jesus redeems us from the bondage of the law:

"But when the fulness of the time was come, God sent forth His Son, made of a woman, made under the law, to redeem them that were under the law, that we might receive the adoption of sons" (Gal. 4:4, 5).

IT HAD TO BE JESUS

God is holy. If God should be anything BUT holy, He would cease to be God. He cannot, He does not, look upon sin. In Romans 3:10-12 we read, "As it is written, There is none righteous, no, not one: There is none that understandeth, there is none that seeketh after God. They are all gone out of the way, they are together become unprofitable; there is none that doeth good, no, not one."

Paul then goes on to describe the condition of the unbeliever: "Their throat is an open sepulchre; with their tongues they have used deceit; the poison of asps is under their lips: Whose mouth is full of cursing and bitterness: Their feet are swift to shed blood: Destruction and misery are in their ways: And the way of peace have they not known: There is no fear of God before their eyes.

"NOW WE KNOW THAT WHAT THINGS SOEVER THE LAW SAITH, IT SAITH TO THEM THAT ARE UNDER THE LAW: THAT EVERY MOUTH MAY BE STOPPED, AND ALL THE WORLD MAY BECOME GUILTY BEFORE GOD. THEREFORE BY THE DEEDS OF THE LAW THERE SHALL NO FLESH BE JUSTIFIED IN HIS SIGHT: FOR BY THE LAW IS THE KNOWLEDGE OF SIN.

"But now the righteousness of God without the law is manifested, being witnessed by the law and the prophets; even the righteousness of God which is by faith of Jesus

Christ unto all and upon all them that believe: for there is no difference: *For all have sinned, and come short of the glory of God;* being justified FREELY by His grace through the redemption that is in Christ Jesus: whom God hath set forth to be a propitiation through faith in His blood, to declare His righteousness for the remission of sins that are past, through the forbearance of God; to declare, I say, at this time His righteousness: that He might be just, and the justifier of him which believeth in Jesus.

"Where is boasting then? It is excluded. By what law? of works? Nay: but by the law of faith. *Therefore we conclude that a man is justified by faith without the deeds of the law"* (Rom. 3:13-28).

In this tremendous passage Paul clearly sets forth the divine fact that all men are sinners — without God, hopeless, helpless, and hell-bound; and by the deeds of the law (*keeping* the law) there shall no flesh be justified. The law could not save, it was not given for that purpose. (*"By the law is the knowledge of sin."*) But the righteousness of God WITHOUT the law IS manifested (present tense) — and of course, *the righteousness of God is Jesus Christ.*

What a holy God demanded, it was imperative that He provide. Only God *could* provide holiness, righteousness, purity and sinlessness. Adam sinned, and *through him,* sin moved upon the entire human family. Like produces like, and therefore the human family could not provide a Saviour. It was imperative that God provide the sinless substitute which He demanded. God cannot — never has and never will — allow sin. The soul that sins is doomed to die.

When Lucifer, "the shining one," thought to overthrow God and exalt his throne above that of the Almighty, God

100

threw him out of heaven and he became the loathsome creature whom we know as the devil — the father of lies, instigator of all that is ugly, all that curses and damns.

God set forth the Lord Jesus Christ, the Lamb without spot or blemish, who shed His blood on the cross. God literally placed Jesus in the womb of the virgin Mary. Jesus was not the product of the human family, He was provided by Almighty God (Luke 1:35).

Since God set forth His only begotten Son — sinless, perfect, foreordained before the foundation of the world; and since the holy, spotless substitute willingly died on the cross and shed His blood for the remission of sin, God can now be *just, righteous, holy* — and yet forgive the unholy and the unrighteous; but this forgiveness is possible only through faith in the shed blood of Jesus. That is the only way God can redeem the sinner.

"Ye shall know the truth, and the truth shall make you free" (John 8:32).

"If the Son therefore shall make you free, ye shall be free indeed" (John 8:36).

"There is a fountain filled with blood drawn from Immanuel's veins;

And sinners, plunged beneath that flood, lose all their guilty stains.

The dying thief rejoiced to see that fountain in his day;

And there may I, though vile as he, wash all my sins away."

Thank God for Jesus, God's only begotten Son, who bore our sins in His own body on the cross, willingly, that we might be redeemed.

101

The following immortal lines were penned by Fanny J. Crosby:

"Redeemed! How I love to proclaim it! Redeemed by the blood of the Lamb;

Redeemed through His infinite mercy, His child, and forever, I am.

Redeemed and so happy in Jesus, no language my rapture can tell;

I know that the light of His presence with me doth continually dwell.

I think of my blessed Redeemer, I think of Him all the day long;

I sing, for I cannot be silent; His love is the theme of my song.

I know I shall see in His beauty the King in whose law I delight;

Who lovingly guardeth my footsteps, and giveth me songs in the night.

Redeemed! Redeemed! Redeemed by the blood of the Lamb;

Redeemed! Redeemed! His child, and forever, I am!"

THERE IS MORE TO COME

We have redemption NOW. We are redeemed from *the curse of sin* NOW. We are redeemed from the *penalty* of sin now, and we are redeemed from the *power* of sin day by day, being kept by the power of God. *Our redemption is in Christ,* through His blood. The forgiveness of sins is according to the riches of His grace—which riches are beyond human understanding.

We are not redeemed with corruptible things; redemption is totally apart from the mind or the hands of man. The precious blood of Jesus, as of a Lamb without blemish and without spot, brings redemption, and *without the shedding of blood is no remission!* Without the blood, judgment is sure; but under the blood we are redeemed from *ALL iniquity.* Under the blood, we are redeemed from the curse and from the bondage of the law — but there is more:

"For we know that the whole creation groaneth and travaileth in pain together until now. And not only they, but ourselves also, which have the firstfruits of the Spirit, even we ourselves groan within ourselves, waiting for the adoption, to wit, THE REDEMPTION OF OUR BODY" (Rom. 8:22, 23).

We are as fully and completely saved this moment as we will ever be, insofar as *the inner man* is concerned. When an unbeliever exercises faith in Jesus Christ, the spirit is redeemed that very moment; but the *body* will be redeemed in the first resurrection: "Behold, what manner of love the Father hath bestowed upon us, that we should be called the sons of God: therefore the world knoweth us not, because it knew Him not. Beloved, now are we the sons of God, and it doth not yet appear what we shall be: but we know that, when He shall appear, we shall be like Him, for we shall see Him as He is" (I John 3:1-3).

"NOW are we the sons of God!" What blessed truth! But it is also true that we groan within ourselves, waiting for *"the redemption of our BODY."* We are sons of God NOW — but we are living in a tabernacle of flesh that causes us to suffer and groan, waiting and longing for that glorious redemption of our body.

When Jesus comes in the Rapture we will receive a glorified body just like His resurrection body. Redemption provides present salvation, but the redemption of the body will occur in that glorious resurrection morning:

"But now is Christ risen from the dead, and become the firstfruits of them that slept. For since by man came death, by man came also the resurrection of the dead. For as in Adam all die, even so in Christ shall all be made alive. But every man in his own order: Christ the firstfruits; afterward they that are Christ's at His coming" (I Cor. 15:20-23).

"Behold, I shew you a mystery; We shall not all sleep, but we shall all be changed. In a moment, in the twinkling of an eye, at the last trump: for the trumpet shall sound, and the dead shall be raised incorruptible, and we shall be changed. For this corruptible must put on incorruption, and this mortal must put on immortality. So when this corruptible shall have put on incorruption, and this mortal shall have put on immortality, then shall be brought to pass the saying that is written, Death is swallowed up in victory. O death, where is thy sting? O grave, where is thy victory? The sting of death is sin; and the strength of sin is the law. But thanks be to God, which giveth us the victory through our Lord Jesus Christ" (Cor. 15:51-57).

"We shall not all sleep." This refers to death of the body, not to unconsciousness of the spirit. We shall not all die, but *we shall all be changed.* At the coming of Christ for His Church, those who have died in the Lord will be raised incorruptible, and those who are alive will be changed "in the twinkling of an eye." This corruptible must put on incorruption, this mortal must put on immortality — and then we will shout, "O grave, where is thy victory! O death, where is thy sting?" The sting of death is sin — but halle-

104

lujah! Jesus removed that sting when He fulfilled the law. The strength of sin is the law — but praise God! Jesus fulfilled every demand of God's holy law. And now we can say, *"Thanks be unto God, which giveth us the victory through our Lord Jesus Christ!"*

I am so glad that our victory comes through the Lord Jesus, and not through our own ability or strength!

I AM NOT AFRAID

I believe that a saved person should KNOW he is saved. Every believer should have the blessed assurance of his salvation, on the basis of God's holy Word. We do not desire to die; we are not anxious to enter the valley of death; we all love life. But born again people should not be *afraid* to die, we should not worry about death. Why? Because Jesus Christ abides in the bosom of every believer, in the Person of the Holy Spirit.

Romans 8:9 tells us, ". . . If any man have not the Spirit of Christ, he is none of His." Romans 8:14 and 16 declare, "For as many as are led by the Spirit of God, they are the sons of God . . . The Spirit itself beareth witness with our spirit, that we are the children of God." In Revelation 1:18 Jesus declares, "I am He that liveth, and was dead; and, behold, I am alive for evermore, Amen; *and have the keys of hell and of death!"*

Jesus — our Saviour, our Redeemer — has the keys of death and the keys of hell. Therefore we should not fear death. We should not fear hell, because we who are redeemed are not going there.

"Redeemed! Redeemed! Redeemed by the blood of the Lamb.

Redeemed! Redeemed! His child, and forever, I am!"

Christianity

CHRISTIANITY

"We preach not ourselves, but Christ Jesus the Lord" (II Cor. 4:5).

Christianity is not a theory *about* Christ. It is not a series of ethical statements proceeding from the *teachings* of Christ. It is not a system built upon the *concept* of Christ. *Christianity IS Christ!*

Christianity is not a cold, formal, dead organization. It is a living organism of which Christ is the living, vital head. If He were taken out of it, it could not survive any more than a *human* body could survive the loss of its head. Christ was God in flesh. He is the head of Christianity, the Saviour of the body — and we are members of His body — we are bone of His bone and flesh of His flesh (Eph. 5:25-30).

Christ — living, dead, buried, and *living again* — is the chief distinction between Christianty and every other religion on earth. *Buddha* is dead, buried, and though he is not risen from the dead, Buddhism survives. *Confucianism* has survived and continued to grow since Confucius died, but there is no record that he ever came back from the grave. The same is true of *Mohammedanism; Christian Science* has continued to grow since the death of its founder, Mary Baker Eddy; and *Russellism* has done wonderfully well without Russell. But if it could be proved that Jesus Christ still lies buried in a tomb in Jerusalem, Christianity would fail because the heart, the soul, *the very essence* of Christianity is CHRIST — not a historical character, not a great man whose body now reposes in a grave in the Holy Land, but THE MAN, CHRIST JESUS — risen, ascended, and now seated at the right hand of God the Father (Heb. 1:1-2; I Tim. 2:5).

Christianity is not just another "religion" nor is it to be

compared with such. Christ is the Incomparable One in that He was born as no other man was ever born (He was conceived by the Holy Ghost) ; He lived as no other man has ever lived (He was sinless) ; and He died as no other has ever died: He simply said, "It is finished!" and then literally took His life in His own hands and handed it back to God! (John 10:17, 18).

In every way, Christ stands as far above other men as the heavens stand above the earth. Christianity is the incomparable religion: no other will compare with it in even a small way.

The Word of God is the only basis for Christianity. Christians do not look to tradition, dogma, or revelation supposedly given to men today. The Word upon which Christianity stands is CHRIST.

In Genesis 3:15 God the Father promised the seed of the woman. From Genesis through Revelation, the Word of God presents the Lord Jesus as the seed who will, at the consummation of all things, personally place Satan in the lake of fire. From Genesis through Revelation the Word of God preaches and presents the Lord Jesus Christ.

After the resurrection of Jesus, two disciples were walking to Emmaus. He joined them, and in the course of the conversation, "... *beginning at Moses and all the prophets, He expounded unto them in all the Scriptures the things concerning Himself.*" You will find the interesting, fast-moving account in Luke 24:13-35.

The entire plan of salvation is summed up in Christ: *God the Father so loved* sinners that *He gave God the son* to make it possible for sinners to be redeemed.

Jesus in a body of flesh obtained pardon for us, and we find pardon *only in His finished work.*

We are saved by the blood of Jesus Christ (I John 1:7; Heb. 9:22; Eph. 1:7).

110

Christ is our sanctification (John 17:17).

We are kept by the power of Christ (I John 1:5).

In Christianity, all that we need is in Jesus — whether it be salvation, sanctification, or victory. We are saved from *sin's curse* through His blood; we are saved from *sin's power* through the leading of the Holy Spirit; and we will be saved from *sin's presence* when Jesus comes in the Rapture.

Regardless of what phase of Christianity we study — whether it be the cross, or Jesus at the right hand of God the Father, or the coming of Christ in the clouds of heaven, the center, soul, and very essence of *every* phase of Christianity is CHRIST.

In Christianity, Christ is the inevitable, inescapable One. He is forever inseparable from THE Faith once delivered to the saints. Apart from the Lord Jesus Christ, everything is lost. Apart from Him there is no light, but all is darkness; apart from Him there is no life — there is only death.

"When Christ, who is our life, shall appear, then shall ye also appear with Him in glory" (Col. 3:4). In Him all things consist; *without* Him, death, darkness, and disaster prevail. Without Christ, men are dead in trespasses and sins. Without Christ, men walk in darkness — and to walk in darkness is certainly to meet disaster.

In the Scripture of our text, Paul says, *"For we preach not ourselves, BUT CHRIST JESUS THE LORD; and ourselves your servants for Jesus' sake."* I have often made the statement that Satan does not care how long, how loud, how sincerely and fervently a minister preaches, just so long as he preaches on a subject apart from Christ and His shed blood. It does not disturb Satan when a man preaches religion, denomination, or self; but when that man preaches Jesus Christ — crucified, buried, and risen, Satan works

111

overtime to blind the minds and the spiritual eyes of unbelievers:

"... If our Gospel be hid, it is hid to them that are lost: in whom the god of this world hath blinded the minds of them which believe not, lest the light of the glorious Gospel of Christ who is the image of God, should shine unto them. For we preach not ourselves, but Christ Jesus the Lord; and ourselves your servants for Jesus' sake. For God, who commanded the light to shine out of darkness, hath shined in our hearts, to give the light of the knowledge of the glory of God in the face of Jesus Christ" (II Cor. 4:3-6). The only message that will break the power of Satan, stop his mouth and deliver a sinner from his grasp is the message of Jesus Christ, the Son of God — crucified, buried, risen again, "according to the Scripture."

The prophets of old preached the Person of Christ without apology: "And He shall send Jesus Christ, which before was preached unto you" (Acts 3:20). They set forth the Lamb, the Messiah, as the only hope of Israel. God's prophets spoke as they were moved by the Holy Ghost, and they gave forth many precious truths concerning Christ's person, His life, His death, His resurrection — and yes, even His return for the Church, and to bring peace on earth, good will toward men.

The Old Testament is filled with the preaching of Jesus Christ. There is no single chapter in all the Bible that has more to say about Jesus than Isaiah 53. And it is hard to understand how any Israelite who has been exposed to that chapter could have missed the Messiah when He came. It is just as unbelievable that people could read the Bible today and see the fulfillment of prophecy all around us, and yet ignore the Christ and refuse the message of God's infallible word.

Not only did the prophets of old preach Christ, but the

Person of Christ was the message of the apostles: "And daily in the temple, and in every house, they ceased not to teach and preach Jesus Christ" (Acts. 5:42). These men had lived with Christ. They not only heard Him preach and teach — they saw Him work miracles, they were daily associated with him in his ministry, and they believed in Him as the Son of God. They witnessed His death, they testified to His resurrection, and they talked with Him frequently during the forty days *following* His resurrection before He ascended back to heaven. They stood on the crest of the Mount of Olives as He ascended and a cloud received Him out of their sight; and then, on the Day of Pentecost, they witnessed exactly what He assured them would come.

Jesus instructed the apostles to tarry in Jerusalem until they should be endued with power from on high; "and when the Day of Pentecost was fully come," they were filled with the Holy Spirit and with great power. Men who had before been weak and fearful, now preached the deity of Christ — His virgin birth, His sacrificial death on the cross, His bodily resurrection — and they boldly declared that He would come again, exactly as He went away! They had a singular message: *CHRIST*.

Later, God called and anointed the Apostle Paul; and when he came on the scene of action, he too preached Christ. The first sermon he ever preached was "Jesus Christ, the Son of God" (Act 9:20).

Paul was an educated man. He was a Judaist, a member of the Sanhedrin. He could have preached on other matters. He was educated at the feet of Gamaliel and he was a master in the religion of the Jews. It was not imperative that he preach Christ; he could have dealt with many subjects and with many aspects of religion. But when Paul became a Christian, a partaker of Christ, he *preached* Christ and *Christ only.* From the moment he was saved until he sealed his testimony with his life's blood, he was jealous for Jesus. He said, "God forbid that I glory, save in the cross! I am what I am by the grace of God. I count all things loss that I might *gain Christ!*"

The person of Christ was the message for the Jew. "Now when they had passed through Amphipolis and Apollonia, they came to Thessalonica, where was a synagogue of the Jews: And Paul, as his manner was, went in unto them, and three sabbath days reasoned with them out of the Scriptures, opening and alleging, that Christ must needs have suffered, and risen again from the dead; and that this Jesus, whom I preach unto you, is Christ" (Acts 17: 1-3).

This was not the message wanted by the Jews. They hated Christ, and Paul would have received much more honor, applause, and praise of men had he stood up in the synagogue and made a few timely remarks on rituals and ethics, a few suggestive hints on economics, or some cutting remarks about the political tyranny and harsh rule of the Caesars. Paul was a free-born Roman Jew, and up to the moment when he met Jesus, he had hated the Christ and all who followed Him.

But He met Jesus on the road to Damascus, met Him face to face; and he knew that the only message that would save the Jews was the message of Jesus — crucified, buried, and risen again "according to the Scriptures." It was this dear apostle who said:

"I say the truth in Christ, I lie not, my conscience also bearing me witness in the Holy Ghost, that I have great heaviness and continual sorrow in my heart. For I could wish that myself were accursed from Christ for my brethren, my kinsmen according to the flesh: Who are Israelites; to whom pertaineth the adoption, and the glory, and the

114

covenants, and the giving of the law, and the service of God, and the promises; whose are the fathers, and of whom as concerning the flesh Christ came, who is over all, God blessed for ever. Amen" (Rom. 9:1-5).

Can you hear the heart-cry of the Apostle Paul on behalf of his people the Jews? Do you grasp the magnitude of his burden for them as he declared that *he would be willing to be cut off from Christ and drop into hell* if by so doing he could save his kinsmen according to the flesh? Yet he knew that the only avenue of salvation for the Jews, as for all others, was the message of Jesus Christ. Therefore *"he preached Christ . . . that He is the Son of God."*

The Person of Christ was the message Philip preached to the Samaritans (Acts 8:5). That was prior to Paul's conversion, and at that time, as Saul of Tarsus, he was playing havoc with the Church and perpetrating severe persecution against believers: "As for Saul, he made havock of the Church, entering into every house, and haling men and women committed them to prison" (Acts 8:3).

"Therefore they that were scattered abroad went every where preaching the Word" (Acts 8:4). These early Christians, even under severe persecution, preached Jesus Christ. ("In the beginning was the Word, and the Word was with God, and the Word was God . . . and the Word was made flesh, and dwelt among us. . ." — John 1:1, 14). They preached the WORD — and the Word was Jesus Christ. Philip was one of those who saw and felt the persecution against the Church. He traveled down to Samaria, and even though the Samaritans were royally hated by the Jews, Philip preached Christ to them and many of them believed and were saved:

"And the people with one accord gave heed unto those things which Philip spake, hearing and seeing the miracles which he did. For unclean spirits, crying with loud voice,

115

came out of many that were possessed with them: and many taken with palsies, and that were lame, were healed, and there was great joy in that city" (Acts 8:6-8). The message of the Person of Christ, preached to the Samaritans, brought salvation to these despised people.

The Person of Christ was the message Paul preached to the Gentiles: "We who are Jews by nature, and not sinners of the Gentiles, knowing that a man is not justified by the works of the law, but by the faith of Jesus Christ, even we have believed in Jesus Christ, that we might be justified by the faith of Christ, and not by the works of the law: for by the works of the law shall no flesh be justified" (Gal. 2:15, 16).

Paul — a free-born Roman Jew, a Pharisee of the Pharisees, having lived *after the straitest sect of the Pharisees* — was called, commissioned, and sent to the hated Gentiles. At the time of the ministry of Jesus and in the days just following His giving of the Great Commission, Gentiles were hated and despised to such great degree that they were often referred to as "dogs." But Paul's meeting with Christ on the Damascus road changed his mind about them. The Lord said of Paul, ". . . He is a chosen vessel unto me, to bear my name before the Gentiles, and kings, and the children of Israel: For I will shew him how great things he must suffer for my name's sake" (Acts 9:15, 16). Paul was not disobedient to the heavenly vision. He obeyed God's call to preach Christ — *"before the Gentiles, and Kings, and the children of Israel."*

God led him to the Athenians, the Bereans, the Thessalonians, the Colossians, the Galatians. He preached to slaves and slaveowners; kings and peasants; elite ladies and women of the streets — but *always* he preached the same message: Jesus Christ — crucified, buried, risen and coming again "according to the Scriptures." He preached

116

the cross and the grace of God — and he had but one message for all.

"Neither is there salvation in any other: for there is none other name under heaven given among men, whereby we must be saved" (Acts 4:12). Paul knew this blessed truth — and he preached it till he died.

There is no more beautiful picture of the message of the Gospel than that found in the sixteenth chapter of Acts. Paul and Silas journeyed to Philippi, and on the Sabbath day they attended a ladies' Bible class which met beside the river:

"And on the Sabbath we went out of the city by a river side, where prayer was wont to be made; and we sat down, and spake unto the women which resorted thither" (Acts 16:13). Paul's message that day was Jesus Christ — He who died on the cross, was buried and rose again for the remission of sin. Lydia, a seller of purple and fine linen, heard that message, she was converted, and she and her entire household were baptized. She then besought Paul and Silas to stay in her home while they were in Philippi. Lydia was Paul's first convert in Europe.

His second convert on this journey was a demented soothsayer who was being used by her masters to get gain. She followed Paul and Silas "for many days," and heard the Gospel as Paul preached day by day. After many days of hearing the message, she received Jesus Christ, she was delivered from her witchcraft — and she ceased to be a way of gain for her masters.

This woman was being used of the devil through witchcraft, and the men to whom she brought gain were greedy after filthy lucre — they cared nothing for her soul. They were simply using her for a tool to make money. Through the message of Jesus Christ — crucified, buried, and risen — this girl was saved. So we step from the elite to the

117

"scum-bum" — from Lydia, a woman of wealth, social position, and influence, to the poor soothsayer who was in bondage to sin, Satan, and her masters who cared only for the profit she brought them.

When these wicked men saw that their hope of gain through the evil arts of this girl had been suddenly ended through her conversion, they seized Paul and Silas, brought them before the magistrates, stirred up the city against them, and had them soundly beaten. *"And when they had laid many stripes upon them, they cast them into prison, charging the jailor to keep them safely: Who, having received such a charge, thrust them into the inner prison, and made their feet fast in the stocks"* (Acts 16:23, 24).

This same Philippian jailer was Paul's third convert in that city. Paul and Silas were locked in the inner cell, their feet securely fastened in the stocks. But at the midnight hour they prayed and sang praises to God. He heard their prayers — and answered with an earthquake that shook the prison, opening all of the doors and loosing the bands of the prisoners. The jailer, waking from sleep and seeing what had happened, naturally supposed his prisoners had fled. He knew that the escape of a prisoner would cost him his life, so he drew his sword and was about to kill himself when Paul cried with a loud voice, "Saying, *Do thyself no harm: for we are all here.*" Then the jailer called for a light, and came trembling before Paul and Silas, and asked, *"Sirs, what must I do to be saved?"*

Notice the question asked by the jailer. He did not ask, "What must I do to become religious?" He did not ask, "What must I do to become a better man?" He asked, "What must I do to be SAVED?" And they said, *"BELIEVE ON THE LORD JESUS CHRIST, and thou shalt be saved, and thy house. And they spake unto him the Word of the Lord, and to all that were in his house."*

Paul and Silas spoke "the Word of the Lord" unto the jailer, and we know that the Word of the Lord is the Gospel. In I Corinthians 15:1-4 we learn that the Gospel is the death, burial, and resurrection of the Lord Jesus — *"according to the Scriptures."*

"And (the jailer) took them the same hour of the night, and washed their stripes; and was baptized, he and all his, straightway. And when he had brought them into his house, he set meat before them, and rejoiced, believing in God with all of his house" (Acts 16:25-34 in part).

Lydia the elite was saved through Paul's message of Christ, crucified, buried, risen; the soothsayer was saved through the same message and she immediately turned from her witchcraft. The wicked, cruel jailer was saved through Paul's message, and immediately took the two men of God to his home and ministered unto them. These three converts were so different in background and walks of life, and yet the same message reached them, melted their hearts, and caused them to be born again through faith in the finished work of Christ.

We today are commanded to preach Jesus Christ, the Son of God. In Mark 16:15 we read, "Go ye into all the world and preach the Gospel to every creature." These are the words of the Lord Jesus as He gave the great commission to the disciples.

In Romans 1:1-3, Paul opens his letter to the Christians at Rome: "Paul, a servant of Jesus Christ, called to be an apostle, separated unto the Gospel of God, (which He had promised afore by His prophets in the holy Scriptures,) concerning His Son Jesus Christ our Lord, which was made of the seed of David according to the flesh."

Every minister of the Gospel is *separated UNTO* the Gospel of God — and woe is me if I preach not the Gospel! The woe of God is upon any minister who does *not* preach the pure Gospel. We are to preach nothing less than Jesus Christ — virgin-born, crucified, buried, risen, ascended, and coming again. We are to add nothing to this message, we are to take nothing from it.

Just before His ascension Jesus said to His disciples, "Ye shall receive power, after that the Holy Ghost is come upon you: and ye shall be witnesses unto me both in Jerusalem, and in all Judaea, and in Samaria, and unto the uttermost part of the earth" (Acts 1:8).

The disciples were to receive power — power to witness, first in Jerusalem, Judaea, Samaria — and then to the four corners of the earth. They were commissioned to witness to a lost world. The only message that will save a sinner is the message of the Gospel, and the Gospel is the death, burial, and resurrection of the Lord Jesus Christ. The curse of God is upon any and all who preach otherwise:

"... But there be some that trouble you, and would pervert the Gospel of Christ. But though we, or an angel from heaven, preach any other gospel unto you than that which we have preached unto you, let him be accursed. As we said before, so say I now again, If any man preach any other gospel unto you than that ye have received, let him be accursed!" (Gal. 1:7-9).

These are solemn, heart-searching words. According to the Scriptures, every false witness — whether he be preacher, teacher, evangelist or layman — is under the curse of Almighty God:

"For I testify unto every man that heareth the words of the prophecy of this book, If any man shall add unto these things, God shall add unto him the plagues that are written in this book: And if any man shall take away from the words of the book of this prophecy, God shall take away his part out of the book of life, and out of the holy city, and from the things which are written in this book" (Rev. 22:18, 19).

There is no respect of persons with God (Rom. 2:11). We are not to add anything TO the Word of God, nor take anything FROM it, lest our part be taken out of the book of life and the plagues of God's judgment be added unto us. We are to preach the pure, unadulterated Gospel — and what IS the Gospel? Paul defined it in his letter to the Corinthians:

"Moreover, brethren, I declare unto you the Gospel which I preached unto you, which also ye have received, and wherein ye stand; by which also ye are saved, if ye keep in memory what I preached unto you, unless ye have believed in vain. For I delivered unto you first of all that which I also received, how that Christ died for our sins according to the Scriptures; and that He was buried, and that He rose again the third day according to the Scriptures" (I Cor. 15:1-4).

The rest of this great chapter in I Corinthians is given over to the resurrection of the Lord Jesus Christ — *bodily;* and to the resurrection of those who die in Christ. It also includes the return of the Lord in the Rapture, referred to in verse 52 as His appearing "in the twinkling of an eye."

These words are understandable. They should be clear to anyone who is not married to a religion or dogma. They simply mean that if any man preach any doctrine which ignores or defames the cross or the bodily resurrection of Jesus, or which denies the resurrection of the saints and the Lord's return in the Rapture, that man is accursed. Paul said, "Woe is me if I preach not the Gospel!"

Jesus Christ came in the flesh — virgin born, very God; He was crucified for the sins of the world, He was buried and the third day He rose again. He ascended into heaven, and He is coming again in the same flesh and bone in which He appeared to the disciples for forty days after His resurrection. Any man who denies any of these tremendous fundamentals of the faith is a deceiver and an antichrist. Such a minister is of the world, and the world will hear him — but true believers will not hear him:

"Beloved, believe not every spirit, but try the spirits whether they are of God: because many false prophets are gone out into the world. Hereby know ye the Spirit of God: Every spirit that confesseth that Jesus Christ is come in the flesh is of God: And every spirit that confesseth not that Jesus Christ is come in the flesh is not of God: and this is that spirit of antichrist, whereof ye have heard that it should come and even now already is it in the world. Ye are of God, little children, and have overcome them: because greater is He that is in you, than He that is in the world. They are of the world: therefore speak they of the world, and the world heareth them. We are of God: he that knoweth God heareth us; he that is not of God heareth not us. Hereby know we the spirit of truth, and the spirit of error" (I John 4:1-6).

"For many deceivers are entered into the world, who confess not that Jesus Christ is come in the flesh. This is a deceiver and an antichrist. Look to yourselves, that we lose not those things which we have wrought, but that we receive a full reward. Whosoever transgresseth, and abideth not in the doctrine of Christ, hath not God. He that abideth in the doctrine of Christ, he hath both the Father and the Son. If there come any unto you, and bring not this doctrine, receive him not into your house, neither bid him God speed: For he that biddeth him God speed is partaker of his evil deeds" (II John 7-11).

These words are final!!! No man has any right to add to or take from the Word of God, nor to make the Word of God *say what he wants it to say* in order to prove his religion or his personal belief. No believer has any right to sit under the ministry of one who has departed from the faith in any way. If you cannot receive a person into your house nor bid him God speed, you certainly should not sit under his preaching!

Bible doctrine does not set one denomination against another. The declaration just quoted from the second epistle of John is placed there in defense of the faith once delivered to the saints, and woe to the man who preaches not the pure Gospel; because according to the Word of God, the judgment of God is upon him — as well as upon *Christians* who support him. (This Scripture in II John refers to rewards — not to salvation.)

What is the message heard from the pulpit of the church you attend? I know I am not the only man who preaches the Gospel — there are thousands of them. God has His faithful winesses today just as He has always had — and *will have* until Jesus comes and the church is caught up to meet Him in the clouds in the air.

Elijah thought he was the only godly man left — but while he was hiding from Jezebel, God reminded him that there were 7,000 faithful prophets who had not bowed the knee to Baal. We are in a sad spiritual plight indeed when we come to the place where we begin to pity ourselves and think we are the only person left who is doing a job for Jesus!

There are many humble pastors and evangelists who preach the Gospel in all of its glorious fullness. There are many missionaries — both on foreign fields and on the home front — who preach the Gospel and *live the Gospel they preach*. But there are also tens of thousands of false teachers and false prophets today.

Any preacher who denies any part of the Gospel is

against Christ, and it is important that born again people belong to and support a church where the pure Gospel is preached. Except in rare instances, anyone who desires to attend a Bible-believing church can do so. It may be necessary to drive several miles on Sunday morning, but I had much rather drive some distance, hear the Gospel and support God's man, than to walk a few steps and support an enemy of Jesus Christ who does not preach the Word of God! If the man where you attend church is not preaching the Gospel, ask God to lead you to some church where you can hear the Word of God preached in all of its purity and power.

For every good thing God has provided, the devil has contrived a cheap counterfeit. God has many ministers whom He has called, ordained, and filled with the Spirit — but the devil also has many false apostles and deceitful workers, ministers of Satan:

"For such are false apostles, deceitful workers, transforming themselves into the apostles of Christ. And no marvel; for Satan himself is transformed into an angel of light. Therefore it is no great thing if his ministers also be transformed as the ministers of righteousness whose end shall be according to their works" (II Cor. 11:13-15).

There are those who maintain that believers should stay in modernistic churches and try to help the situation; but I remind you that God's Word says we are to have no fellowship with the unfruitful works of darkness:

"Be ye not unequally yoked together with unbelievers: for what fellowship hath righteousness with unrighteousness? and what communion hath light with darkness? And what concord hath Christ with Belial? or what part hath he that believeth with an infidel? And what agreement hath the temple of God with idols? for ye are the temple of the living God; as God hath said, I will dwell in them, and walk in them; and I will be their God, and they shall be my people. Wherefore come out from among them, and be ye separate, saith the Lord, and touch not the unclean thing; and I will receive you, and will be a Father unto you, and ye shall be my sons and daughters, saith the Lord Almighty" (II Cor. 6:14-18).

"... Have no fellowship with the unfruitful works of darkness, but rather reprove them" (Eph. 5:11). According to these passages, we are to come out from among them, we are to have no fellowship with them — but that is not enough: We are also to REBUKE these false teachers.

Jude speaks of these teachers of error, these lying prophets, in his little epistle of only one chapter:

"Likewise also these filthy dreamers defile the flesh, despise dominion, and speak evil of dignities. Yet Michael the archangel, when contending with the devil he disputed about the body of Moses, durst not bring against him a railing accusation, but said, The Lord rebuke thee. But these speak evil of those things which they know not: but what they know naturally, as brute beasts, in those things they corrupt themselves. Woe unto them! for they have gone in the way of Cain, and ran greedily after the error of Balaam for reward, and perished in the gainsaying of Core. These are spots in your feasts of charity, when they feast with you, feeding themselves without fear: clouds they are without water, carried about of winds; trees whose fruit withereth, without fruit, twice dead, plucked up by the roots; raging waves of the sea, foaming out their own shame; wandering stars, to whom is reserved the blackness of darkness for ever. And Enoch also, the seventh from Adam, prophesied of these, saying, Behold, the Lord cometh with ten thousands of His saints, to execute judgment upon all, and to convince all that are ungodly among them of all their ungodly deeds which they have ungodly committed, and of all their hard speeches which ungodly sinners have spoken against Him. These are murmurers, complainers, walking after their own lusts; and their mouth speaketh great swelling words, having men's persons in admiration because of advantage. But, beloved, remember ye the words which were spoken before of the apostles of our Lord Jesus Christ; how that they told you there should be mockers in the last time, who should walk after their own ungodly lusts. These be they who separate themselves, sensual, having not the Spirit" (Jude 8-19).

We are saved by grace through faith minus works. "Not by works of righteousnesses which we have done," because all of our righteousness are as filthy rags; but Jesus is made unto us wisdom, righteousness, sanctification, and redemption. He who knew no sin was made sin, that we in Him might be made the righteousness of God. What the law could not do because of the weakness of the flesh, Jesus did in a body of flesh; in that body He conquered the world, the flesh, and the devil. And then, after His crucifixion, He conquered the grave and rose again!

"...If thou shalt confess with thy mouth the Lord Jesus, and shalt believe in thine heart that God hath raised Him from the dead, thou shalt be saved" (Rom. 10:9).

We are redeemed wholly through the finished work of Jesus Christ, but we will be rewarded according to our faithful stewardship. We should therefore be careful what we do, what we say, where we go, how we conduct our daily lives — and what kind of minister and church we support!

"For other foundation can no man lay than that is laid, which is Jesus Christ. Now if any man build upon this foundation gold, silver, precious stones, wood, hay, stubble; Every man's work shall be made manifest: for the day shall declare it, because it shall be revealed by fire; and the fire shall try every man's work of what sort it is. If any man's work abide which he hath built thereupon, he shall receive a reward. If any man's work shall be burned, he shall suffer loss: but he himself shall be saved; yet so as by fire" (I Cor. 3:11-15).

If I had a thousand hands, I would raise them all for Jesus! If I had ten thousand tongues to sing His praise, I would use them all to say, "Thank God for Jesus, my Saviour!" But that is not enough: When I come to the end of life's journey, I want some trophies to lay at His feet when we crown Him Lord of all. I want to be a good, faithful steward. I want my life to count for Jesus. How about YOU?

In closing, let me emphasize once more: *Salvation is free.* Redemption is in Christ Jesus. Christianity is CHRIST in YOU. Salvation is the gift of God, not of works; but *rewards are earned.* To become a son of God is free — Jesus paid it all; but to be a disciple is costly. Through faith in the finished work of Jesus I am a son of God — but I want to be a good disciple.

Christ and Our Salvation

CHRIST AND OUR SALVATION

"But of Him are ye in Christ Jesus, who of God is made unto us wisdom, and righteousness, and sanctification, and redemption: That, according as it is written, He that glorieth, let him glory in the Lord" (I Cor. 1:30-31).

For many glorious years I have been preaching the Gospel of the marvelous Grace of God; but the more I read the Bible and the more I attempt to preach the Word in all of its fullness and power, the more I see and understand that Jesus is the Hub of the Wheel of salvation, and all of the spokes are connected to Him. In this message which the Lord has laid on my heart I will attempt to show you what I mean by the statement, "All the spokes in the wheel of salvation are connected to the Hub . . . the Lord Jesus."

1. In the first place, I want to point out that salvation from sin and everlasting hell is a gift. If there is anything taught in the Word of God clearly enough to be understood by man, it is the fact that **salvation is God's Gift** to hell-deserving mankind! I do not believe any person who knows anything at all about Scripture, or who has attended Church and Sunday school very many times in his life, will deny this verse: "For God so loved the world, that He gave His only begotten Son, that whosoever believeth in Him should not perish, but have everlasting life" (John 3:16). That verse is often referred to as "The Gospel in a nutshell." That verse clearly states that God so loved the world that He GAVE His only begotten Son . . . and the reason for the giving of the Son is that we might have everlasting life through the gift of God (His Son, the Lord Jesus). That is **a settled fact.**

131

But beloved, before any person can receive a gift, it matters not the nature or the value of the gift, the person to receive that gift must first know about it. There must be knowledge, there must be wisdom. One cannot receive the Lord Jesus Christ as his personal Saviour if that person has not heard about the Lord Jesus, and if that person does not know what the Bible says about sinners being saved from their sins. In the very outset of this message let me point out that it is absolutely imperative for the sinner to have knowledge concerning God's gift . . . God's sacrifice . . . in order that he might be saved. Where does this knowledge begin?

"The fear of the Lord is the beginning of knowledge" (Prov. 1:7). I have traveled in every continent on earth except one, preaching the Gospel, testifying to the power of God . . . but I have never been any place on the face of this earth, even in the deepest, darkest jungle, but that I have found the people fear some great deity whom they believe they will meet after death! It is true that the heathen do not know the true and living God. Many of them worship snakes, trees, monkeys, the moon, stones . . . they have all kinds of gods. But down deep in their hearts, they know there is some kind of Great Being somewhere beyond this life. **When such persons have the opportunity to hear the Gospel,** many of them (not all, but many of them) put their faith and trust in the Lord Jesus Christ. I have pointed this out to prove a point:

The Bible declares, "The Heavens declare the glory of God, and the firmament showeth His handiwork" (Psalm 19:1). The Psalmist uttered these words many, many years before the birth of Christ, and then after Jesus came and gave His life a ransom for sinners, Paul gives us a little more light on the subject: "For the wrath of God is revealed from Heaven against all ungodliness of men, who hold the truth in unrighteousness; because that which may be known of

God is manifest in them; for God hath shewed it unto them. For the invisible things of Him from the creation of the world are clearly seen, being understood by the things that are made, even His eternal power and Godhead; so that they are without excuse: Because that, when they knew God, they glorified Him not as God, neither were thankful; but became vain in their imaginations, and their foolish heart was darkened. Professing themselves to be wise, they became fools, and changed the glory of the uncorruptible God into an image made like to corruptible man, and to birds, and four-footed beasts, and creeping things. Wherefore God also gave them up to uncleanness through the lusts of their own hearts, to dishonour their own bodies between themselves: Who changed the truth of God into a lie, and worshipped and served the creature more than the Creator, Who is blessed forever. Amen" (Romans 1:18-25).

In these verses, Paul clearly testifies that the reason we have heathen today, and the reason there are multiplied millions who know nothing of God, is because when they knew God, they refused to glorify Him as God; they were unthankful, they became vain in their thinking, and **God gave them up.** However, they are without excuse because "the invisible things of Him from the creation of the world are clearly seen, being understood by the things that are made, even His eternal power and Godhead. So they are without excuse."

I have had the privilege of speaking to people who have never heard the name of Jesus Christ. I remember on one occasion I spoke through an interpreter to the Pygmies away back in the French section of Africa, and a dear woman came forward and in Pygmy language asked the missionary, "If what this man has said about Jesus is true, why has not someone told us long before now?" That Pygmy woman bowed on her knees, and the missionary led her to a saving knowledge of Jesus Christ.

The fear of the Lord is the starting place of salvation. Sinners will never come to God nor call upon God for salvation until first they **fear** God. I do not mean that they are **afraid of God**, but that they fear Him because they know they must meet Him, and that He will give to them justice in that Great Judgment Day. To fear God in the true sense of the word, spiritually, is to desire to know more about God, how to approach God, how to please God, and **how to be saved.**

Let me point you to these words in our text: "But of Him are ye in Christ Jesus, Who of God is made unto us WISDOM . . ." (I Cor. 1:30a). In this verse Christ is made unto us wisdom, righteousness, sanctification, and redemption . . . four things. But please notice the Holy Spirit did not say, "Christ is made unto us redemption, sanctification, righteousness and wisdom." No, no!! WISDOM first . . . and then we become righteous when we believe on the Lord Jesus Christ and receive Him as our personal Saviour; then sanctification is progressive in that the more we learn about Jesus, the more we dedicate our lives to Him, the more completely we are sanctified unto God . . . that is, **set apart FOR God**, and for God's glory . . . even every member of our bodies. Then of course, in the final analysis we are redeemed completely when we stand before Him and receive our glorified bodies, and hear Him say, "Enter thou into the joys of thy Lord." I do not mean that we are not saved the split second we put our faith in Jesus . . . WE ARE! The moment we trust Him, we are just as saved as we will ever be. But our redemption will not be fully complete until we stand in His presence and receive our glorified body. (Please read I John 3:1, 2).

When we hear about God, when we know that we must meet God and from His hand receive our just reward, if we are normal we will have a sensation in our inner man that will cause us to fear meeting the Great God who controls this universe and everything in it. When that fear is created in our heart, we will long to hear a minister or a teacher . . . or to read for ourselves what the Bible tells us about God. For instance, let me illustrate: If we have severe pains in our abdomen, and we have wondered many times if we have chronic appendicitis, we will find our way to the family doctor for an examination, fearing that our appendix may one day rupture and like many others in days past and gone, we will die because of poison and gangrene. Now that may be a crude illustration . . . but nevertheless it is true. If we feel that we have some dreaded disease, it creates a fear; we go to a doctor to learn the truth. When a sinner really recognizes the fact of God, that fact will stir the sinner's heart and cause him to fear. If the sinner follows the impulse of the inner man, he will seek to find out more about God and how to meet Him in peace, instead of in fiery judgment.

There is only one place to find the truth about God . . . and that one place is in His Word. Paul tells us, "Let God be true and every man a liar" (Rom. 3:4). "Verily, verily, I say unto you, He that heareth my word, and believeth on Him that sent me, hath everlasting life, and shall not come into condemnation: but is passed from death unto life" (John 5:24). In this glorious verse John tells us that if we hear the word, and believe on the God Who sent Jesus, we have everlasting life, and will not come into condemnation but that we have passed from death unto life. The only place where we may get the wisdom or the knowledge to receive the Lord Jesus and to become the possessor of this salvation is from God's Holy Word. In Paul's writings to the young ministers and to the churches, he always cries out, "Hear the Word!" "Study the Word!" "Believe the Word!" "Receive the Word!" "But continue thou in the things which thou has learned, and hast been assured of, knowing of whom thou hast learned them; and that from a child thou hast known the Holy Scriptures, which are able to make thee wise unto salvation through faith which is in Jesus Christ" (II Timothy 3:14-15).

Please notice the statement "**The Holy Scriptures which are able to make thee wise unto salvation.**" Paul preached Christ, and Him crucified. Words like these are recorded by Paul as the Holy Ghost dictated the Holy Scriptures to him. "I am determined not to know anything among you save Jesus Christ and Him crucified." Again, "God forbid that I should glory, save in the cross of the Lord Jesus Christ."

Hear Paul as he cried out to the believers at Corinth: "Moreover brethren, I declare unto you the Gospel which I preached unto you, which also ye have received, and wherein ye stand; by which also ye are saved, if ye keep in memory what I preached unto you, unless ye have believed in vain. For I delivered unto you first of all that which I also received, how that Christ died for our sins according to the Scriptures; and that He was buried, and that He rose again the third day according to the scriptures" (I Cor. 15:1-4). Paul clearly declared to the believers in the church at Corinth, "I preached unto you the Gospel. You received it, by which you are saved. The Gospel that I delivered to you is the Gospel that I received . . . that is, that Christ died for our sins **according to the Scriptures . . .**" Please notice: not "according to the Baptists," not "according to the Methodists," not "according to the Holiness" but "ACCORDING TO THE SCRIPTURES." Paul goes on to say that Christ was "buried **according to the scriptures;** He rose **according to the scriptures.**" Paul had a singular message . . . namely, **The Scriptures.** He did not preach one thing at any time during his ministry except what the scriptures clearly taught. Oh, that we had more Pauls today! Men who would stick to the word of God, and preach the word of God, and not preach dogma, tradition, and denominationalism. This poor world is starving for the pure, unadulterated word of God.

"If any man lack wisdom, let him ask of God, that giveth to all men liberally, and upbraideth not; and it shall be given him" (James 1:5).

In this verse of Scripture, we are clearly taught that wisdom comes from God. I am talking about TRUE wisdom . . . PURE wisdom. Of course, men do go to school to train the mind . . . and I am afraid more emphasis is being put on minds today than on souls, even in our schools that are supposed to be Christian . . . schools that are training the ministers of tomorrow. True wisdom, pure wisdom, true knowledge, pure knowledge come only from God . . . the wisdom that brings salvation. We cannot believe right, we cannot think right about Jesus, until we hear what the Bible has to say about Him. God gives the wisdom with which and through which we receive Jesus Christ as our personal Saviour, and this wisdom comes only from God through His precious Word; because after all, "In the beginning was the Word, and the Word was with God and the Word WAS God" (John 1:1). You cannot separate the Word and God, nor the Word and Christ, nor the Word, Christ, and God . . . they are One and the same in salvation, redemption, sanctification and eternal salvation.

In the years that I have been preaching the Gospel, I have learned a few things by experience. I do not believe there has ever been a case of genuine salvation apart from Godly fear. I do not believe that any sinner will call on God for redemption until that sinner fears God in his (or her) heart. Godly fear worketh repentance . . . and I do not believe there has ever been a case of true repentance toward God apart from Godly fear. Do not forget: "The fear of the Lord is the beginning of knowledge." A sinner cannot THINK right about God, cannot BELIEVE right about God, and cannot PRAY right TO God, until that sinner has heard the Word that brings wisdom **about** God.

2. In the second place, let me answer THE question that is asked by almost every unsaved person who expresses an interest in salvation. The question is: "How is a sinner saved? How do we get salvation? How do we become a Christian?"

This question needs a **Bible answer.** If you ask the Jew, he will give you **his** answer. If you ask a Protestant, he will give you **his** answer. If you ask a Roman Catholic he will give you **his** answer. If you ask God Almighty, He will give you the **Bible answer.** "Let God be true, and every man a liar" (Rom. 3:4).

The jailer at Philippi asked the question, "Sirs, what must I do to be saved?" (Acts 16:30-31). Paul and Silas said to the jailer, "Believe on the Lord Jesus Christ and thou shalt be saved, and thy house." Please notice the next verse: "And they SPAKE UNTO HIM THE WORD OF THE LORD, and to all that were in his house" (Acts 16:32). You remember a little while ago I said Paul had a singular message... Christ crucified, buried, risen **according to the Scriptures.** So when the jailer asked, "What must I do to be saved?" Paul answered with the Scriptures.

There is so much ignorance among people, even among church members, concerning salvation. Many times preachers, Sunday school teachers, laymen, refer to salvation as "it" or "something" or as "church membership." But salvation is not "it," "something," "church membership," "baptism"... salvation IS A PERSON: "Salvation is of the Lord." Do not forget our text ... "Christ is made unto us wisdom, righteousness, sanctification, redemption." Anything pertaining to salvation, any part of salvation, is Jesus, and JESUS ALONE. There is not one thing that any man can do to add to the statement made by the Son of God on the cross, "IT IS FINISHED!" (John 19:30). Jesus Christ satis-

138

fied every demand of God. Jesus Christ paid it all . . . He finished the work the Father sent Him to do . . . and the Father sent Him to give His life a ransom for sinners. So salvation is of the Lord; salvation IS the Lord! I am sure that you want other scriptures to prove the point that I have just stated. I will be very happy to give them to you:

"For by grace are ye saved through faith; and that not of yourselves: it is the gift. of God: not of works, lest any man should boast" (Ephesians 2:8-9).

Paul declares in these verses that we are saved by grace, and Jesus is grace (John 1:14). So if we are saved by Grace, then we are saved by Jesus. This saving grace becomes ours by faith . . . but where do we get the faith?

"So then, faith cometh by hearing, and hearing by the Word of God" (Romans 10:17). "In the beginning was the Word, and the Word was with God and the Word was God" (John 1:1). "And the Word became flesh and dwelt among us and we beheld His glory as of the glory of the only begotten of the Father, full of grace and full of truth" (John 1:14). So you see, the Word, Jesus, and Jesus on earth are synonymous; Jesus in the flesh was The Word made flesh. The Word took up its abode in Jesus, in a body of flesh, and Jesus brought salvation down to man.

"Not by works of righteousness which we have done, but according to His mercy He saved us by the washing of regeneration and the renewing of the Holy Ghost" (Titus 3:5). Not by right works that we do, but **"according to His mercy"** He saves us, by the washing of regeneration and the renewing of the Holy Ghost. But how are we regenerated? Christ is made unto us redemption, and certainly redemption and regeneration are Siamese twins as having to do with our salvation.

Perhaps someone is saying . . . not aloud, but in your heart . . . "Mr. Greene, I have never seen Jesus, and I do not know of anyone of my loved ones or friends who has ever seen Jesus. And how can I believe on Him and receive Him, never having seen Him?" The answer is, "FAITH." "Faith is the substance of things hoped for, the evidence of things not seen" (Heb. 11:1). Kind friend, anything that I can see, feel, or taste I do not need any faith to accept. I have never seen Jesus — but I rejoice in Him with joy unspeakable and full of glory (I Peter 1:8). Read that glorious verse in your Bible. Faith does not ask to see nor feel. Faith accepts, faith believes, without seeing or feeling . . . without some gigantic, emotional experience! If we are saved by "feelings" then it is not by faith. If we are saved by sight then it is not by faith; because faith is substance that we cannot see; faith is evidence that we have never seen. We know that He lives, because the Word of God tells us that He lives — and do not forget: "Let God be true, and every man a liar."

The devil has been trying to destroy this Bible ever since God spoke and man wrote down what He uttered; but the Bible shines as it has never shone before, and there are more people who believe this Book than ever before. I realize there are many, many more people on earth than ever before, and certainly that contributes to the statement that there are more real, born-again Christians on earth today than ever before, in spite of the fact that there are billions of sinners who do not know God! I know that you can produce hypocrites . . . church members who are not what they ought to be; but every time you produce a hypocrite, I will produce a real, genuine, child of God who proves by daily living that he is a child of God. In spite of the fact that I have never seen God, and I have never talked with God face to face, and I have never had my hands on God as I place my hands on my child, or as I feel the touch of my wife, I know that GOD IS, because many years ago even though I could not see Him, I believed in Him; I received His Christ, and Jesus came into my heart and He lives there.

Paul puts it this way: "Christ in you, the hope of glory" (Col. 1:27). And again, "Ye are dead, and your life is hid with Christ in God" (Col. 3:3). And again: "Ye are complete in Him" (Col. 2:10). So even though I cannot see Him, I cannot put my hands on Him, I cannot call Him up on the telephone, I know He lives! You ask me how I know He lives? **He lives within my heart!**

There is only ONE WAY to be saved: "Believe on the Lord Jesus Christ and thou shalt be saved" (Acts 16:31).

3. In the third place, I am sure someone is asking, "But Mr. Greene, how do you KNOW that you are saved, and how can I know that I am saved?" Time and space will not permit me to answer that question fully in this message, but I will give you enough scriptural answer to satisfy your heart, if you will only believe it:

"He that believeth on the Son of God hath the witness in himself: he that believeth not God hath made Him a liar; because he believeth not the record that God gave of His Son. And this is the record, that God hath given to us eternal life, and this life is in His Son. He that hath the Son hath life, and he that hath not the Son of God hath not life. These things have I written unto you that believe on the Name of the Son of God; that ye may know that ye have eternal life, that ye may believe on the Name of the Son of God" (I John 5:10-13). Read these verses from your own Bible.

"He that believeth on the Son hath the witness in himself." That is scripture . . . ("Let God be true, and every man a liar!") When you **believe** on the Lord Jesus Christ and put your **trust** in the Lord Jesus Christ, He puts in your heart the witness of the Holy Spirit.

"The Spirit Himself witnesseth with our spirit that we are the sons of God" (Romans 8:16). Notice the next statement: "And this is the record, that God hath given unto us eternal life, and this life is in His Son." Please notice, beloved:

"This life is IN HIS SON" . . . that is, **Jesus.** Salvation is not in the church, in the baptistry, in good works, in giving, in going, in doing, in abstaining, in quitting; but salvation is **of the Lord,** salvation is IN JESUS and our eternal life is in God's Son, the Lord Jesus Christ.

"He that hath the Son, hath life; and he that hath not the Son, hath not life." That is very clear and plain. If you receive Jesus, you have everlasting life. Receive Him by faith, and He puts the Witness in your heart . . . "These things have I written unto you that believe on the Name of the Son of God, that ye may KNOW that ye have eternal life, and that ye may believe on the Name of the Son of God" (I Jno. 5:13). These scriptures, God's Holy Word, are written that we might believe on the Lord Jesus Christ, and believing on the Lord Jesus Christ have everlasting life, because everlasting life is in Jesus. And when we believe on Him, and receive Him, we have everlasting life.

In closing this message, let me say there are three ways that I know I am saved:

a. The first great reason I know I am saved is that God TELLS me I am saved. Here is what I mean: "Verily, verily, I say unto you, he that heareth my Word and believeth on Him that sent me **hath everlasting life** and shall not come into condemnation but is passed from death unto life" (John 5:24). I have heard the Word, believed the Word, received the Word . . . and God said that if I would do that, He would save me and God cannot lie!

Hear this: "That if thou shalt confess with thy mouth the Lord Jesus and shalt believe in thine heart that God hath raised Him from the dead, thou shalt be saved" (Romans 10:9). I have done that. I have confessed with my mouth Jesus as my Lord; I believe in my heart that God raised Him from the dead. God's Holy Word tells me that if I will do that, He will save me. So I know I am saved because God's Word tells me I am saved — and God cannot lie!

b. In the second place I know I am saved because the Holy Spirit witnesses in my heart:

"And the Spirit Himself witnesseth with our spirit that we are the sons of God" (Rom. 8:16). Down deep in my heart I know I am saved because I have the witness of the still, small voice of the Holy Spirit in my heart. The moment I put my trust in Jesus, God put in my bosom the Holy Spirit, and He has been there ever since that moment, and thank God He will remain there, because I am sealed until the day of redemption (Read Eph. 4:30). Please read this very carefully — and then turn back to Romans 8 and read verse 9. I know I am saved because the Holy Spirit witnesses with my spirit that I am a child of God.

c. In the third place, I know I am saved because my heart . . . my own God-given conscience . . . the "inner man" . . . tells me that I am saved:

"And hereby we know that we are of the truth and shall assure our hearts before Him. For if our heart condemn us, God is greater than our heart and knoweth all things. Beloved, if our heart condemn us not, then we have confidence toward God" (I John 3:19-21). I wish you would turn in your own Bible and read these glorious verses. When I lie down at midnight, at 1:00 o'clock or 2:00 o'clock in the morning; or when I waken at 4:00, 4:30, or 5:00 o'clock, I thank God that I have the assurance in my heart that I am saved. I have been at death's door two times in the last three years, and I can truthfully say that I faced the Grim Reaper and the Valley of the Shadow with no fear, because my heart did not condemn me. I am not perfect; I am a man; I live in a body of flesh; I fall short of God's glory . . . but I am saved by His grace, I am kept by His power . . . I am assured by His Word and I am unafraid to die! I would not give you two cents for a salvation that does not take the fear of dying out of you. "Fear hath torment; he that feareth hath not been made perfect in love." Read I John 4:18-19.

Let me close this message by simply saying to you that if you ever hear God Almighty say "Well done ... enter thou into the joys of thy Lord," it will be because you put your faith in the Lord Jesus. The statement is, "Enter thou into the joys of thy Lord." And if Jesus is not your Saviour and Lord, you will never enter that Celestial City. God said, "This is my beloved Son in whom I am well pleased. Hear Him." God wants us to hear His Son, believe His Son, receive His Son, trust in His Son, because in Jesus we are complete (Col. 2:10). It was Jesus who said, "Father, it is finished!"

The Second Blessing

THE SECOND BLESSING

"And, being assembled together with them, commanded them that they should not depart from Jerusalem, but wait for the promise of the Father, which, saith He, ye have heard of me. For John truly baptized with water; but ye shall be baptized with the Holy Ghost not many days hence" (Acts 1:4 and 5).

"For in Him dwelleth all the fulness of the Godhead bodily. And ye are complete in Him, which is the head of all principality and power" (Col. 2:9, 10).

Is there a specific teaching in the Word of God that there is a definite second work of grace after one becomes a believer? This is the question which naturally arises in the hearts of many believers when they think in such terms as being *baptized* with the Holy Ghost, being *filled* with the Holy Ghost, or the *infilling* of the Holy Ghost.

Some believers tell us that when we are born we receive all that God has to give us. "In Christ we receive all there is," they say. Others teach that there is a definite time after conversion when a person comes to the point of either going deeper with God, or gradually "cooling off" spiritually. Both teachings are correct to a degree.

A careful study of the New Testament proves beyond the shadow of a doubt that every believer possesses the Holy Spirit. From the second we believe on Christ, we can enjoy the presence of the Spirit of God within our hearts:

"But ye are not in the flesh, but in the Spirit, if so be that the Spirit of God dwell in you. Now if any man have not the Spirit of Christ, he is none of His" (Rom. 8:9).

147

Also in the Word of God we read where on several occasions the disciples were FILLED with the Spirit. To the believers at Ephesus Paul said, ". . . Be not drunk with wine, wherein is excess; but be filled with the Spirit" (Eph. 5:18). From this verse of Scripture it seems that since it is a sin to get drunk on wine, it is also a sin not to be filled with the Spirit. And since these words were written to believers, it seems reasonable and Biblical that it is possible to be born again, thus possessing the Spirit by His presence, and yet not be FILLED with the Spirit. I personally believe the Bible teaches that to *have* the Spirit is one thing, and to be *filled* with the Spirit is quite another thing.

When Jesus appeared in the upper room after His resurrection (where the disciples were hiding for fear of the Jews), He breathed on them and said, "Receive ye the Holy Spirit." By this we know that the disciples possessed the Holy Spirit before Pentecost, but on the Day of Pentecost they were *baptized* in the spirit or *filled with the Spirit,* and this experience completely changed their ministry and their power in soul winning.

It is true that "in Him dwelleth all the fulness of the Godhead bodily . . . Ye are complete in Him,which is the head of all principality and power . . .and God hath blessed us with all spiritual blessing IN CHRIST." On the other hand, no one will deny that the majority of believers are just ordinary, nominal Christians. Only a few enter into the spiritual birthright of every believer which is the fullness of the Spirit, the fullness of Christ, and abundant life with a cup running over, spreading blessings to all with whom they come in contact.

One of the greatest needs of the Church today is that God's ministers go back to the New Testament teaching concerning the ministry of the Holy Spirit in the lives of believers in this dispensation:

The Holy Spirit convicts us of sin (John 16:7-9).

Apart from Him we cannot come to Christ (John 6:44).

Through the power of the Holy Spirit we are born into God's family (John 3:13 and 14).

We possess the Holy Spirit (Rom. 8:9)

We are led by the Spirit (Rom. 8:14).

We are assured by the Spirit (Rom. 8:16).

We are sealed by the Spirit until the day of redemption (Eph. 4:30). But these facts do not outlaw the teaching of God's Word: *"Be ye FILLED with the Spirit."*

THERE ARE MANY "SECOND BLESSINGS" IN THE SPIRITUAL LIFE

1. *Christ's death for us—our death with Christ*:

Christ died in our stead. He bore our sins in His own body on the cross—and He did it willingly:

"Who His own self bare our sins in His own body on the tree, that we, being dead to sins, should live unto righteousness: by whose stripes ye were healed (I Pet. 2:24).

"Therefore doth my Father love me, because I lay down my life, that I might take it again. No man taketh it from me, but I lay it down of myself. I have power to lay it down, and I have power to take it again. This commandment have I received of my Father" (John 10: 17, 19).

Jesus voluntarily went to the cross. He threw Himself into the waters of judgment and sank beneath the awful weight of the judgment of our sin, that WE might find

149

peace in the storm of God's eternal wrath. He stilled the waves of judgment that would have swallowed us; He provided a rest that no one else could have provided. All that Adam lost in the Garden of Eden, Jesus redeemed on the Mount of Calvary. He came to take our place, He died in our stead.

However, as we study the New Testament we see clearly that Jesus not only died as our substitute, but we who are believers *died with Him*. God reckons us dead when we believe on the Lord Jesus Christ. Before we believe on Him we are dead in sin, but when we believe, we share His death:

"For ye are dead, and your life is hid with Christ in God" (Col. 3:3).

"I am crucified with Christ: nevertheless I live; yet not I, but Christ liveth in me: and the life which I now live in the flesh I live by the faith of the Son of God, who loved me, and gave Himself for me" (Gal. 2:20).

Jesus bore our sins in His own body on the cross. Through His death God reckons us dead with Him. In HIM we have answered for our sin, and sin has no further claim upon us. Since He paid the sin-debt in full, the Holy Spirit emphasizes the divine fact that sin is not only answered for in a penal sense, but it no longer has any dominion over us. Whereas we were slaves and bondservants of sin, now we are to reckon ourselves a corpse—DEAD to sin and to all that it demanded from us:

"Likewise reckon ye also yourselves to be dead indeed unto sin, but alive unto God through Jesus Christ our Lord" (Rom. 6:11).

Christ did in flesh what we could never have done in the flesh, and what the law could never have done because of the *weakness* of the flesh. Because of the victory Christ won in His death, WE have victory over sin because we are dead *with Christ*.

"Behold, what manner of love the Father hath bestowed upon us, that we should be called the sons of God: therefore the world knoweth us not, because it knew Him not. Beloved, now are we the sons of God, and it doth not yet appear what we shall be: but we know that, when He shall appear, we shall be like Him; for we shall see Him as He is" (I John 3:1-3).

2. *The second blessing of peace*:

Because of the death of Jesus we have peace WITH God and we enjoy the peace OF God. Peace WITH God depends entirely upon God. He made peace by the blood of Jesus Christ: "And, having made peace through the blood of His cross, by Him to reconcile all things unto Himself; by Him, I say, whether they be things in earth, or things in heaven. And you, that were sometime alienated and enemies in your mind by wicked works, yet now hath He reconciled in the body of His flesh through death, to present you holy and unblameable and unreproveable in His sight" (Col. 1:20-22). Hell-deserving sinners receive the benefit of peace with God through personal faith in the finished work of the Lord Jesus Christ: "Therefore being justified by faith, we have peace with God through our Lord Jesus Christ" (Rom. 5:1).

In the Garden of Eden, fellowship between God and man was broken when Adam deliberately disobeyed God. God told him that he might eat freely of every tree in the Garden with the exception of the tree of the knowledge of good and evil. He was not to eat of the fruit of that particular tree, and God spelled out to him the ultimate results if he should disobey. But Satan tempted Eve, she ate—

151

and then she gave to Adam and HE ate. At that moment, peace between God and man was broken, fellowship was severed, enmity was declared.

Up to the Man Christ Jesus, no man had ever been able to satisfy God. The law could not satisfy Him because of the weakness of the flesh (Rom. 8:1-3). But Jesus took a body (study the tenth chapter of Hebrews) and in that body He did what no man had ever done or ever *could* do. What God demands, God provides, and only a holy God *could* provide redemption. Peace with God is ours by faith in the finished work of the Lord Jesus Christ, not by any degree of merit on the part of man.

The peace OF God is enjoyed by those rare believers who are anxious in nothing, prayerful in everything, thankful for everything, not weary in well doing, looking unto Jesus the author and finisher of our faith, seeking first His kingdom and knowing that all needful things will be added. These are the peculiar believers who enjoy their spiritual birthright. When believers meet God's divine conditions, God keeps His promise: "Thou wilt keep him in perfect peace, whose mind is stayed on thee: because He trusteth in thee" (Isa. 26:3). "And the peace of God, which passeth all understanding, shall keep your hearts and minds through Christ Jesus" (Phil. 4:7).

Jesus came that we might have life and have it abundantly. There is no place in faith for anxiety, worry, or fear. If God be for us, who can be against us? He who spared not His own beloved Son, will He not also *through HIM* freely bestow upon us all things? Yes, He is able to do exceeding abundantly above anything we think or ask.

"Peace I leave with you, my peace I give unto you: not as the world giveth, give I unto you. Let not your heart be troubled, neither let it be afraid" (John 14:27).

3. *The second blessing of salvation and holiness*:

Our salvation is instantaneous when we believe on the Lord Jesus Christ and He redeems us; but we are to grow in grace—not INTO grace, for we are BORN INTO grace; but we grow IN grace after we are saved. The grace of God brings salvation, brings us into our ark of safety (the Lord Jesus) where we are safe from the flood waters of the damned and the hurricanes of hell. The Word of God assures us that we are saved and safe in Christ; we are made to sit together in heavenly places in Christ Jesus (Eph. 2:6).

Salvation is totally of grace, ALL grace, works excluded:

"There is therefore now no condemnation to them which are in Christ Jesus, who walk not after the flesh, but after the Spirit. For the law of the Spirit of life in Christ Jesus hath made me free from the law of sin and death" (Rom. 8:1, 2).

"Not by works of righteousness which we have done, but according to His mercy He saved us, by the washing of regeneration, and renewing of the Holy Ghost; which He shed on us abundantly through Jesus Christ our Saviour" (Titus 3:5,6).

"For by grace are ye saved through faith; and that not of yourselves: it is the gift of God: not of works, lest any man should boast" (Eph. 2:8, 9).

Salvation is grace, pure grace, self and works excluded —but salvation does not stop there: *Holiness* is daily consecration and separation unto the holy One, that He in HIS holiness may dwell in us, and through us reproduce the holiness of His character in our daily living. There is only one brand of Bible holiness, and that is *Christ completely permeating our lives.* It is not enough to practice the *negative* side of holiness; we must also abide in the *positive* side. Jesus Christ is our holiness, He is made unto us wisdom, righteousness, sanctification, redemption, and we are complete in Him; but we *reproduce God's holiness* only as we surrender unreservedly to Jesus and allow Him to display God's righteousness and holiness in what we do and how we live in relationship to our fellowman:

"Be ye not unequally yoked together with unbelievers: for what fellowship hath righteousness with unrighteousness? and what communion hath light with darkness? And what concord hath Christ with Belial? or what part hath he that believeth with an infidel? And what agreement hath the temple of God with idols? for ye are the temple of the living God; as God hath said, I will dwell in them, and walk in them; and I will be their God, and they shall be my people. Wherefore come out from among them, and be ye separate, saith the Lord, and touch not the unclean thing; and I will receive you and will be a Father unto you, and ye shall be my sons and daughters, saith the Lord Almighty" (II Cor. 6:14-17).

"Having therefore these promises, dearly beloved, let us cleanse ourselves from all filthiness of the flesh and spirit, perfecting holiness in the fear of God" (II Cor. 7:1). By the blood of the Paschal Lamb, which pointed to the Lord Jesus Christ, God saved His people on the night the death angel passed through Egypt; but He did more than that: He also gave instructions concerning the tabernacle, that God Himself might dwell among His people. The same holds true in the experience of the child of God today. We are saved from the wrath of God and from

154

eternal hell by the blood of Jesus Christ. We are saved for Christ's sake, to God's glory, that the Lord may be sanctified in our hearts in His own will and sovereign sway (I Pet. 3:15).

I confess that the doctrine of holiness has been abused by some, but what other sacred doctrine of Christianity has NOT been abused? We cannot afford to ignore the Bible teaching of holiness just because it has been misinterpreted and abused by a minority, because the Word of God distinctly tells us that without holiness no man shall see the Lord (Heb. 12:14). But we cannot produce holiness by self-righteousness or through the works of the flesh. We can be holy only as we yield to Jesus. We must yield our bodies a living sacrifice and our members as instruments of righteousness unto the Lord.

4. *The second blessing of forgiveness and cleansing*:

The death of Jesus Christ not only provides forgiveness —it also provides cleansing. Forgiveness of our sins is the act of God in mercy, whereby He blots out our sins because of the shed blood of the Lord Jesus Christ who bore our sins in His own body, thus satisfying the holiness of God. Because of His shed blood, God sets us free from the penalty and the power of sin which held us as unbelievers, rendering us bondslaves through the weakness of the flesh.

"Forgiveness" means more and goes deeper than *"pardon."* If you will study the New Testament carefully you will discover that the word "pardon" is not used once, but "forgiveness" is used frequently. A man may be in the penitentiary, serving a just sentence for murder. After a few years, on the basis of good conduct or some other extenuating circumstance, the governor and the parole

155

board can grant a pardon to that man—but they cannot forgive the murder he committed.

Jesus accomplished that which man could never accomplish: He does not PARDON—HE FORGIVES; and when Jesus Christ, through the blood of His cross, forgives our sins, we stand in His presence and in the presence of God as though we had never committed a sin. God forgives us for Christ's sake (Eph. 4:32). To the Israelites in Egypt, God said, "When I see the blood I will pass over you." So it will be when we stand before Him on that great day. "...Without shedding of blood is no remission" (Heb. 9:22). Apart from the blood of Jesus Christ there is no forgiveness.

The blood of Jesus makes it possible for God to be just, and yet justify the ungodly sinner who puts his trust in the shed blood of Jesus: "Being justified freely by His grace through the redemption that is in Christ Jesus: whom God hath set forth to be a propitiation through faith in His blood, to declare His righteousness for the remission of sins that are past, through the forebearance of God; To declare, I say, at this time His righteousness: that He might be just, and the justifier of Him which believeth in Jesus" (Rom. 3:24-26). But the blood of Jesus provides much more:

The blood of Jesus Christ takes care of any sin or mistake that the true believer makes AFTER God initially forgives our sins: "But if we walk in the light, as He is in the light, we have fellowship one with another, and the blood of Jesus Christ His Son cleanseth us from all sin" (I John 1:7).

"My little children, these things write I unto you, that ye sin not. And if any man sin, we have an Advocate with the Father, Jesus Christ the righteous: And He is the

156

propitiation of our sins: and not for our's only, but also for the sins of the whole world" (I John 2:1, 2).

The blood of Jesus Christ cleanses us from *all sin.* It not only takes care of the initial sin that would damn us, but it also takes care of the sins that would rob the Christian of reward. If we DO sin, breaking fellowship with our heavenly Father and the Lord Jesus Christ, we have an Advocate—Jesus Christ the righteous One. He is our atonement, He stands in our stead before God in all of His holiness and He pleads our case. For Christ's sake, God forgives, cleanses, and keeps us day by day, moment by moment. When God looks at the believer, He sees the blood that covers the sinful heart, and in His eyes we are just as pure, clean, and holy as the blood of Jesus that covers us.

5. *The second blessing of "us in Christ—Christ in us":*

When Jesus bore our sins in His own body on the cross, through His shed blood He made it possible for *us* to abide in *Him*; and when we believe on Him, *He* abides in US. Writing to the Corinthian Church, Paul said "I knew a man IN CHRIST above fourteen years ago . . ." Paul definitely designates believers as being *"in Christ."* Writing to the Romans He said, "There is therefore now no condemnation to them which are IN CHRIST JESUS" (Rom. 8:1).

To the Colossians he said, "If ye then be risen with Christ, seek those things which are above, where Christ sitteth on the right hand of God. Set your affection on things above, not on things on the earth. For ye are dead, and your life is hid with Christ in God" (Col. 2: 1 :3).

In Ephesians 2:6 Paul Tells us, ". . . And hath raised us up together, and made us sit together in heavenly places IN CHRIST JESUS."

To the Corinthians he declared that all believers are baptized into one body, and that body is Christ: "For as the body is one, and hath many members, and all the members of that one body, being many, are one body: so also is Christ. For by one Spirit are we all baptized INTO one body, whether we be Jews or Gentiles, whether we be bond or free; and have been all made to drink INTO one Spirit" (I Cor. 12: 12-13).

Not only are we IN CHRIST—which fact is glorious and marvelous; but CHRIST IS IN US: " . . . Christ in you, the hope of glory" (Col. 1:27).

In Galatians 2:20 Paul said, "I am crucified with Christ: nevertheless I live; yet not I, but *Christ liveth in me*: and the life which I now live in the flesh I live by the faith of the Son of God, who loved me, and gave Himself for me." The divine position of the born again person is that he is in Christ, in all the perfection of Christ's work, and the eternal worth of the Lord Jesus Christ. And because we now occupy such a position, Christ should be in the believer in all of His fullness. He should occupy every member, even to the least; and every detail of our daily living and thinking should be permeated by Him. Christ should be in the believer in all the potentiality of His holiness, His righteousness, and His beautiful character.

We can be epistles read of men, but only as we allow Christ to occupy every secret chamber of our heart and soul; only as we allow Him to lead in all that we do.

6. *The second blessing of the life in Christ Jesus*:

In Jesus we have life—but we have the *second* blessing of life *more abundant*: ". . . I am come that they might have life, and that they might have it more abundantly" (John 10:10).

To be saved, one must believe on the Lord Jesus Christ, and all who believe on the Lord Jesus Christ are saved; but not all who are saved enjoy their spiritual birthright. God withholds no good thing from them who walk uprightly—but if we sow sparingly, we shall reap sparingly. Throughout the New Testament we are instructed to let our light shine, rather than hiding it under a bushel. We are told to use our talents to bless others, we are to be "the salt of the earth."

In I Corinthians 3:11-15 Paul tells us in understandable language that there is such a thing as going to heaven without a reward:

"For other foundation can no man lay than that is laid, which is Jesus Christ. Now if any man build upon this foundation gold, silver, precious stones, wood, hay, stubble; every man's work shall be made manifest: for the day shall declare it, because it shall be revealed by fire; and the fire shall try every man's work of what sort it is. If any man's work abide which he hath built thereupon, he shall receive a reward. If any man's work shall be burned, he shall suffer loss: but he himself shall be saved; yet so as by fire."

That person who is saved but whose stewardship is lost will also experience great loss while here upon this earth—not the loss of his soul, but loss of spiritual blessings—joy that comes through service, and abundant living produced by full surrender. Jesus came not only to save us and give us eternal life, but that we might have life more abundantly.

We might use as an example the woman who followed Jesus one day and was healed of an issue of blood which had troubled her for twelve years. This woman was alive, yet for twelve long years she had suffered and sought help in vain. She did not have physical life in its abundance. But Jesus delivered her and gave her abundant life. Whether or not she followed Him after that, the Scripture does not say, but I personally believe she did. I believe Jesus healed her physically and saved her soul.

Using this as an example, I suggest that some of you have perhaps been suffering from the disease of sin for many years — twelve, twenty, forty, or fifty years. Perhaps you have tried all kinds of religions, you have joined several churches, perhaps you have written to several radio preachers for literature. But instead of getting better, you have grown worse all the time. Come to Jesus! He will save you—and then, if you will allow Him, He will not only give you *life,* He will give you life *abundantly.*

Even many of *God's children* are weighted down with spiritual disease, crippled by spiritual paralysis, and the only way to be cured of these ailments which rob the Christian of his usefulness is to come to Jesus and let Him deliver from that which holds you in bondage and causes you not only to suffer personally, but also causes the kingdom of God to suffer through your inconsistency! If you are a believer you are either drawing men TO God, or driving them further FROM Him. It is costly to live on the borderline, to follow Jesus afar off; but how rewarding it is to get into the yoke with Jesus and walk with him as He directs us, step by step.

The only way to enjoy our spiritual birthright is to yield soul, spirit, and body unreservedly unto the Lord: "And the very God of peace sanctify you wholly; and I pray God your whole spirit and soul and body be preserved blameless unto the coming of our Lord Jesus Christ" (I Thess. 5:23).

7. *The second blessing of rest*:

Jesus said, "Come unto me, all ye that labour and are heavy laden, and I will give you rest. Take my yoke upon you, and learn of me; for I am meek and lowly in heart: and ye shall find rest unto your souls" (Matt. 11:28, 29).

In these marvelous verses we have a twofold rest:

(a) Jesus said, *"Come unto me,"* and that simple invitation is to "whosoever will." He *invites*—and then He *promises*: "I will give you REST." Please notice, He says, "I will GIVE you rest." The promised rest is a gift, bound by no conditions except that we come unto HIM; and when the sinner comes to Jesus with a heart and life full of weariness and unrest, *Jesus gives him rest.*

(b) But notice the last part of the promise: "YE SHALL FIND REST UNTO YOUR SOULS." Jesus gives rest to the heart when we come unto Him for salvation; but when we take His yoke upon us, when we walk with Him in the yoke and learn of Him as we feed upon His Word day by day, we find *daily* rest, *hourly* rest, unto our souls.

In Jesus we have rest in our hearts because we know our sins are forgiven, covered by the blood, and forgotten. We know that He will never leave us nor forsake us, He will go with us all the way, even to the end. We have twofold rest, because we rest in the divine fact that our sins are forgiven and forgotten, and also in the present fact that we are kept by His power as we walk in the yoke with Him, learning more about Him as we study His Word.

8. *The second blessing of being made meet for our spiritual inheritance*:

We are admonished to give thanks unto the Father, "which hath made us meet (sufficient) to be partakers of the inheritance of the saints in light" (Col. 1:12). We are made meet for our inheritance only because of God's act of grace. It is only IN CHRIST that we are accepted by God for the inheritance eternal.

Please notice that it is GOD who makes us acceptable. We do not condition ourselves to the sufficiency. We are made partakers of the inheritance through the divine act of a loving God, on the merit of the finished work of the Lord Jesus Christ. Paul urges Timothy to be "a vessel unto honour, sanctified, and meet for the master's use, and prepared unto every good work" (II Tim. 2:21).

No believer is meet for the Master's use unless he is sanctified and wholly dedicated unto the Lord. A vessel defiled is unfit for God's use. The Lord uses the servant who is completely yielded to Him, consecrated to carrying out His extraordinary work here on earth. God wants us to enjoy the fulness of grace, which is our spiritual birthright; but if we refuse to yield our members as instruments of righteousness and our body a living sacrifice, wholly sanctified and blameless, then God cannot give into our hands the service that would bring the greatest blessing to humanity, the greatest glory to God, and the greatest reward to US.

Is is not wonderful? Who but a loving God would take a poor, wretched, miserable sinner and make him fit for the inheritance of the riches of God, and then allow him to become a vessel unto honor, used of Jehovah God! God could have used holy angels or spotless cherubim to carry out His work on earth—but HE chose to use man; and those who will yield to Him, live a sanctified life, cleansed and made a vessel unto honor, He makes meet for His use. It is glorious to be a son of God—but it is MORE glorious to realize that God allows us to be His servants here upon earth to do for Him what He could have commissioned angels to do.

9. *The second blessing of acceptance*:

We are made sons IN THE SON OF GOD: "To the praise of the glory of His grace, wherein He hath made us *accepted in the Beloved*" (Eph. 1:6). "There is therefore now no condemnation to them which are *IN Christ Jesus . . .*" (Rom. 8:1). As many as receive Jesus, God "borns" them into heaven's family, making us saints in the Holy One: "And ye are complete in Him, which is the head of all principality and power" (Col. 2:10). Completeness is God's best. JESUS was God's best, given for earth's worst. We who are believers are beloved IN the Beloved. We are heirs of God, joint-heirs with Christ the Beloved Son. In the true meaning of the Greek word "accepted," we are *"much graced"* of God when we are accepted in the Beloved. We are placed in a position that is totally unmerited and undeserved and we are placed there because of God's grace.

The practical results of being accepted in the Beloved is expressed by Paul in II Corinthians 5:9: "Wherefore we labour, that, whether present or absent we may be accepted of Him." In this verse, Paul is thinking of that day when all believers will appear at the judgment seat of Christ to receive the rewards for things done in the body. If we build upon the foundation (the Lord Jesus Christ) gold, silver, and precious stones, we will receive a reward; but if we build wood, hay, and stubble, we will see our works burned and will suffer loss.

The uppermost desire of every believer should be to hear Jesus say, "Well done, thou good and faithful servant." But if we hope to hear those words, we must apply ourselves, yield to His will, and present ourselves to the Lord in an acceptable way. Cain brought the fruit of the ground, produced by the labor of His own hands from the earth which God had cursed. Abel brought the firstling of his flock, and Paul tells us, "By faith Abel offered unto God a more excellent sacrifice than Cain, by which he obtained witness that he was righteous, God testifying of his gifts: and by it he being dead yet speaketh" (Heb. 11:4).

It was not because Abel was a better man than Cain that God accepted his offering, but because Abel's offering was a blood sacrifice—that which was not produced by the labor of his own hands nor from the ground which God had cursed. We must let go and let God have His wonderful way in our heart and life if we hope to be acceptable to Him.

10. *The second blessing of union (which is communion)* :
Every born again child of God is united to Christ, who is the Head of all believers: "For by one Spirit are we all baptized into one body, whether we be Jews or Gentiles, whether we be bond or free; and have been all made to drink into one Spirit" (I Cor. 12:13).

"For we are members of His body, of his flesh, and of His bones" (Eph. 5:30).

"Now therefore ye are no more strangers and foreigners but fellow-citizens with the saints, and of the household of God; and are built upon the foundation of the apostles and prophets, Jesus Christ Himself being the chief corner stone; In whom all the building fitly framed together groweth unto an holy temple in the Lord: In whom ye also are builded together for an habitation of God through the Spirit" (Eph. 2:19-22).

To be in unity of the Spirit is to enjoy everything in common with the Lord Jesus Christ. It is to know the joy of His presence, the exceeding joy of His companship, every moment of every hour of every day. It is to know the helpfulness and the all-sufficiency of His presence. "What shall we then say to these things? If God be for us, who can be against us?" (Rom. 8:31).

11. *The second blessing of the Holy Spirit*: *adoption and power*:

We are born of the Spirit: "Jesus answered, Verily, verily, I say unto thee, Except a man be born of water and of the Spirit, he cannot enter into the kingdom of God (John 3:5).

We are led by the Spirit: "For as many as are led by the Spirit of God, they are the sons of God" (Rom. 8:14).

We are sealed by the Spirit: "And grieve not the Holy Spirit of God, whereby ye are sealed unto the day of redemption" (Eph. 4:30).

But writing to the Christians at Rome, Paul declares that they had the *Spirit of adoption*:"For ye have not received the spirit of bondage again to fear; but ye have received the Spirit of *adoption*, whereby we cry, Abba, Father. The Spirit itself beareth witness with our spirit, that we are the children of God: and if children, then heirs; heirs of God, and joint-heirs with Christ . . . " (Rom. 8:15-17).

To the Galatians Paul wrote, "But when the fulness of the time was come, God sent forth His Son, made of a woman, made under the law, to redeem them that were under the law, that we might receive *the adoption of sons*. And because ye are sons, God hath sent forth the Spirit of His Son into your hearts, crying, Abba, Father. Wherefore thou art no more a servant, but a son; and if a son, then an heir of God through Christ" (Gal. 4:4-7).

But the Galatians were not walking in the Spirit. Paul

observed their shallow testimony, their mediocre steward-ship, and he longed in his heart that Christ might be form-ed in them and that they might so walk (Gal. 4:19).

No one can deny the Bible doctrine that it is altogether possible to be born of the Spirit and yet not be filled with or possessed by the Spirit. It is one thing to be a child of God through the Power of the Spirit (we are drawn to God by the Spirit, convicted by the Spirit, and born by the Spirit) ; but it is altogether another thing to be an obedient, yielded, Spirit-filled child of God.

I am not referring to *a second work of grace.* We are SAVED by God's grace, and no person can be *partially* saved. When we are saved by God's grace, we are entirely and eternally saved; but salvation and stewardship, sal-vation and reward, salvation and surrender, are not one and the same. Some people do fully surrender the mo-ment they are born again; others do not. Therefore, to possess the Spirit of God in the new birth is not necessarily to be possessed BY the Spirit. God has made it possible for us to enjoy a twofold blessing: We receive the Spirit when we are born again, but it is our spiritual birthright to be totally possessed and led by the Holy Spirit.

12. *The second blessing of being "made nigh" unto God*:

It is true that believers are "made nigh" through the miracle of the new birth and the power of the shed blood; but we are also admonished to "draw near." When the sinner hears the Gospel and is convinced of sin, and through the convicting power of the Holy Spirit that sinner be-lieves on the Lord Jesus Christ, he is "made nigh by the blood of Christ" (Eph. 2:13). But this is not the extent or fulness of our spiritual experience. In Hebrews 10:19-22 we read:

"Having therefore, brethren, boldness to enter into the

holiest by the blood of Jesus, by a new and living way, which He hath consecrated to us, through the veil, that is to say, His flesh; and having an high priest over the house of God; *Let us draw near with a true heart in full assurance of faith,* having our hearts sprinkled from an evil conscience, and our bodies washed with pure water."

The poor sinner is an alien from God, blinded by the god of this age, totally depraved, dead in trespasses and sins, and is by nature a child of the devil. When such a creature recognizes the need of a Saviour and from the heart believes unto salvation through the shed blood of Jesus, that poor, wretched, hell-deserving sinner is made nigh unto God through the precious blood of Jesus—and " . . . the blood of Jesus Christ His Son cleanseth us from all sin" (I John 1:7).

Then when we are saved, we are invited to enter boldly into the holy of holiness—which is a most remarkable privilege. In the Old Testament it was sudden and certain death for any person to go behind the veil into the holy of holies, except the high priest appointed by Jehovah God; and he entered once each year—first with blood for his own sin, and then with blood for the sins of the people. But since Calvary, when the blood of Jesus Christ was poured out on the cross for the remission of sin, we are invited to enter boldly into the holy of holies by "a new and living way."

13. *The twofold blessing of: Being SEALED BY the Spirit, and FILLED WITH the Spirit:*

The Holy Spirit *convicts us of sin*—John 16:7-9.

The Holy Spirit *draws us to God*—John 6:44.

The moment we believe, we are *born* of the Spirit— John 3:5.

Believers *possess* the Spirit—Rom. 8:9.

Believers are *led* by the Spirit—Rom. 8:14.

The Spirit gives unshakeable *assurance*—Rom. 8:16.

And then—*believers are SEALED by the Spirit*: "And grieve not the Holy Spirit of God, whereby ye are sealed unto the day of redemption" (Eph. 4:30). "In whom ye also trusted, after that ye also heard the word of truth, the Gospel of your salvation: in whom also after that ye believed, ye were sealed with that Holy Spirit of promise, which is the earnest of our inheritance until the redemption of the purchased possession, unto the praise of His glory" (Eph. 1:13-14).

Yet these very same believers to whom Paul wrote those words, were also exhorted by him to be FILLED with the Spirit: "And be not drunk with wine, wherein is excess; but be filled with the Spirit" (Eph. 5:18).

The Holy Spirit is God's seal, His mark of ownership, denoting that the believer is His property, purchased and paid for at the tremendous price of the shed blood of Jesus. But to be *filled* with the Spirit is to enjoy the abundance of God's grace and the abundant life Jesus speaks of in John 10:10.

To be filled with the Spirit, one must be entirely emptied of all else. The Spirit-filled life never displays the flesh; only the Spirit is seen. Whatever the Spirit-filled believer may do, he will do it all to the glory of God, for the Spirit came—not to speak of Himself, but to glorify the Lord Jesus Christ. God the Father said, "This is my beloved Son in whom I am well pleased". If we hope to please God the Father we must glorify God the Son; and the only way we can glorify God the Son as we should, is to be *filled with the Spirit*.

There is only one way to become a child of God. There are many religions but only ONE salvation: "But as many as received Him, to them gave He power to become the sons of God, even to them that believe on His name: Which were born, not of blood, nor of the will of the flesh, nor of the will of man, but of God" (John 1:12, 13).

We become children of God by receiving Christ as Saviour by faith; however, Jesus said to His disciples, "But ye shall receive power, after that the Holy Ghost is come upon you: and ye shall be witnesses unto me both in Jerusalem, and in all Judaea, and in Samaria, and unto the uttermost part of the earth" (Acts 1:8).

For any believer who studies God's Word with an open heart and an open mind forgetting denominational tradition and dogma, there is no question as to the truth that it is altogether possible to receive Jesus and be born of the Spirit, and yet not possess the power of testimony. There are a few who completely surrender to God the moment they are saved, but with the majority of Christians God's call to service and the believer's complete surrender TO that call comes at a later date—sometimes days, sometimes weeks, maybe months — and sometimes YEARS — after conversion.

Wholehearted consecration and complete separation from the world unto the Lord is not a second work of grace: *it is a complete yielding.* In other words, it is literally flinging ourselves at the feet of Jesus and saying from the the heart:

"Have thine own way, Lord! Have thine own way!
　　Thou art the Potter, I am the clay.
Mould me and make me after thy will,
　　While I am waiting, yielded and still.

Have thine own way, Lord! Have thine own way!
  Search me and try me, Master, today!

Whiter than snow, Lord, wash me just now,
  As in thy presence humbly I bow.

Have thine own way, Lord! Have thine own way!
  Wounded and weary, help, me I pray!

Power—all power—surely is thine!
  Touch me and heal me, Saviour divine!

Have thine own way, Lord! Have thine own way!
  Hold o'er my being absolute sway!

Fill with thy Spirit till all shall see
  Christ only, always, living in me!"

It is interesting to note that Jesus pointed out that the world cannot receive the Holy Spirit: "Even the Spirit of truth; whom the world cannot receive, because it seeth Him not, neither knoweth Him: but ye know Him; for He dwelleth with you, and shall be in you" (John 14:17).

However, rivers of living water are promised to all who believe on the Lord Jesus Christ from the inner man: "He that believeth on me, as the Scripture hath said, out of his belly shall flow rivers of living water. (But this spake He of the Spirit, which they that believe on Him should receive: for the Holy Ghost was not yet given; because that Jesus was not yet glorified.)" (John 7:38, 39).

When Jesus appeared to the disciples in the upper room, He breathed on them and said, "Receive ye the Holy Ghost" (John 20:22). He then promised that they should receive power after the Holy Ghost should come upon them, and this pointed to Pentecost. I repeat: This is not a "second work of grace," but the receiving of the fullness of the Spirit for the power we need in order to witness, win souls, and preach the Gospel to the ends of the earth—yea, to every creature.

On the Day of Pentecost, all that were in the upper room were *baptized* in the Holy Ghost, but as we read the book of Acts we find many occasions where the disciples were *filled* with the Holy Spirit. We know, therefore, that there is *ONE baptism*, but *many FILLINGS*. A believer receives the Spirit only one time. In this dispensation of grace the Holy Spirit does not come upon men and depart from them as in the Old Testament era when He anointed individuals for specific ministries, and then *departed* from them. In this dispensation of Grace, the Holy Ghost came on the Day of Pentecost, He will remain until the Rapture, and every born again believer possesses the Holy Spirit—but sad to say, not every born again believer is possessed BY the Holy Spirit. The great need in the church today is for believers to be filled, empowered, and fully controlled by the Holy Spirit, thus being effective witnesses and soul winners.

I cannot overemphasize the fact that all believers possess the Holy Ghost. There is no mistake about this divine Bible fact. Any person who does not possess the Holy Spirit is not saved. However, "the FULLNESS of the Spirit" is not necessarily the same as *receiving* the Spirit.

The Word of God does not leave us in darkness nor in doubt as to what it means to be filled with the Spirit. There are many occasions in the Word of God where the fullness of the Spirit is spoken of and the result of the fullness of the Spirit are indicated. No one can worship as he should *apart from* the fullness of the Spirit. In Luke 1:41 we read that Elizabeth was filled with the Holy Ghost, and she blessed God in the devotion of her spirit. She truly worshipped "in spirit and in truth."

171

Our testimony cannot be fully effective unless we are filled with the Spirit. Zacharias was filled with the Holy Ghost (Luke 1:67), and prophesied concerning the mission of the Lord Jesus Christ here upon this earth. No believer is fully equipped to be an effective servant and soul-winner until he knows the fullness of the Spirit. Christ Himself was full of the Holy Spirit (Luke 4:1), and on the Mount of Temptation He was victorious when the devil hurled at Him every test hell could afford.

The minister, the missionary, the teacher, the layman cannot speak with spiritual authority unless filled with the Holy Spirit.

The disciples of Jesus were commanded to tarry until they were endued with power, and they were all filled with the Holy Spirit (Acts 2:4). And in the fullness of the Spirit, controlled entirely by the Spirit and under His absolute sway, they spake as the Spirit gave them utterance (Acts 2:4).

Those who are filled with the Holy Spirit enjoy spiritual boldness. We see the disciples, so fearful before Pentecost, but AFTER Pentecost, filled with the Holy Spirit, they declared the Word of God with boldness (Acts 4:31). These disciples who faced imprisonment and death for the sake of the Gospel were the same disciples who trembled and hid before Pentecost!

No man should allow himself to be elected to the office of deacon or steward unless he can testify that he possesses the fullness of the Spirit. The first deacon in the New Testament Church was Stephen, ". . . a man full of faith and of the Holy Ghost . . . and Stephen, full of faith and power, did great wonders and miracles among the people . . . But he, being full of the Holy Ghost, looked up sted-

172

fastly into heaven, and saw the glory of God, and Jesus standing on the right hand of God" (Acts 6:5, 8; 7:55, 56). Because he was filled with the Spirit, Stephen spoke with boldness, even though it cost him his life. Because he was filled with the Spirit, he could see beyond, into the very presence of God Himself, and as the angry crowd stoned him to death, he prayed, "Lord, lay not this sin to their charge!" (Acts 7:60).

True spiritual thankfulness and appreciation can never be ours apart from the fulness of the Spirit. Barnabas is an example. He was full of the Holy Spirit and was thus able to appreciate God's work and miracles through others: "For he was a good man, and full of the Holy Ghost and of faith: and much people was added unto the Lord" (Acts 11:24).

As never before, in this day and hour, we who are workers together with the Lord, spreading the Gospel of the grace of God in this dark hour, need spiritual discernment. Jesus warned against false teachers, false apostles, false preachers, and we cannot know these false teachers apart from spiritual discernment. Paul was filled with the Holy Ghost, and he was not ignorant of the devil's wicked devices.

"Then Saul, (who also is called Paul,) filled with the Holy Ghost, set his eyes on him, and said, O full of all subtilty and all mischief, thou child of the devil, thou enemy of all righteousness, wilt thou not cease to pervert the right ways of the Lord?" (Acts 13:9, 10).

Believers, filled with the Spirit, can face all of life's anxieties. We can face all of our spiritual duties, and fulfill those duties in a manner pleasing to the Lord—but ONLY through the fullness of the Spirit. Thus believers are admonished, "And be not drunk with wine, wherein is excess; but be filled with the Spirit" (Eph. 5:18).

Just as leprosy is a type of sin in the Old Testament, and the leper is a type of the sinner, so is oil a type of the Holy Spirit. Oil was used at the cleansing of the leper and at the consecration of the priest. In Leviticus 2:5 and 6 we read, "And if thy oblation be a meat-offering baken in a pan, it shall be of fine flour unleavened, mingled with oil. Thou shalt part it in pieces, and pour oil thereon . . ."

In Leviticus 2:4 we read, "And if thou bring an oblation of a meat-offering baken in the oven, it shall be unleavened cakes of fine flour *mingled* with oil, or unleavened wafers *anointed* with oil."

Please notice that the oil was to be *mingled with fine flour*. The fine flour is a type of new nature, which is the product of the Holy Spirit. Jesus said to Nicodemus, "Except a man be born of the Spirit . . . he cannot see the kingdom of God." In John 1:12-13 we read, " . . . As many as received Him, to them gave He power to become the sons of God, even to them that believe on His name: Which were born . . . of God."

Notice in Leviticus 2:4 and 5 the oil was to be mingled with the fine flour. The Hebrew word translated "mingled" means to mix thoroughly in order that the oil become part of that with which it is mixed, and thus the oil and the fine flour become one.

In Leviticus 2:6, oil was to be *poured* on the offering. The Hebrew word here translated "pour" means literally "to pour out," and the picture here implies "to melt metal and pour it out upon an object until the metal becomes hard, or is firm." The same word used in I Kings 7:24

174

is translated "cast," denoting a foundry where the metal is melted and poured into the mold, thus casting different figures or tools. In Job 41:23 the word is translated "firm," and in Job 11:15 it is translated "stedfast." So we see that the oil and the fine flour are mixed until they become one, and then the oil is poured upon the mixture to make it firm and stedfast. This is the picture of a consecrated Christian, totally possessed by the Holy Spirit.

The Hebrew word "anointed" means *to rub with oil.* In Jeremiah 22:14 the same word is translated "painted." In the Old Testament this word is often used in connection with setting apart individuals to preach or teach, or unto sanctification, as in Exodus 29:36: "And thou shalt offer every day a bullock for a sin-offering for atonement: and thou shalt cleanse the altar, when thou hast made an atonement for it, and thou shalt *anoint it, to SANCTIFY it."*

Isaiah said, "The Spirit of the Lord God is upon me; because *the Lord hath anointed me* to preach good tidings unto the meek; he hath sent me to bind up the broken-hearted, to proclaim liberty to the captives, and the opening of the prison to them that are bound; to proclaim the acceptable year of the Lord, and the day of vengeance of our God; to comfort all that mourn" (Isa. 61:1).

Do you see the beautiful picture? The word "anointed" means to rub with oil—or, in our present day language, it would be *to paint,* as we paint a surface. We do not think of the paint and the surface as two separate objects, because the paint becomes part of the object painted. Thus it is when the Spirit of God anoints us. When the Spirit is poured out upon us, He is mingled with our inner man and we become ONE in Christ Jesus—we are in Him, He is in us. We then possess divine nature, we sit

175

in heavenly places in Christ Jesus, we are dead and our lives are hid with Christ in God; and *He who IS our life* indwells us in the Person of the Holy Spirit.

Thus when we see the words "mingled," "poured," and "anointed" in their typical application, the truth becomes evident that the Spirit permeates the life He has begotten unto salvation, that He may form our character in firmness and in holiness, and thus fit us for divine service.

In the cleansing of a leper, two things were imperative: *blood,* and *oil.* The blood was sprinkled upon the leper, upon different members of his body, and thus he was cleansed and sanctified (Lev. 14: 1-12). This is typical of two things taught in the espistle to the Hebrews: First, *the heart sprinkled from an evil conscience,* and second, the *entire being sanctified unto the Lord*:

"How much more shall the blood of Christ, who through the eternal Spirit offered Himself without spot to God, purge your conscience from dead works to serve the living God?" (Heb. 9:14).

"Let us draw near with a true heart in full assurance of faith, having our hearts sprinkled from an evil conscience, and our bodies washed with pure water" (Heb. 10:22).

"Wherefore Jesus also, that He might sanctify the people with His own blood, suffered without the gate. Let us go forth therefore unto Him without the camp, bearing His reproach. For here have we no continuing city, but we seek one to come. By Him therefore let us offer the sacrifice of praise to God continually, that is, the fruit of our lips giving thanks to His name. But to do good and to communicate forget not: for with such sacrifices God is well pleased. Obey them that have the rule over you, and submit yourselves: for they watch for your souls, as they that must give account, that they may do it with joy, and not with grief: for that is unprofitable for you" (Heb. 13:12-17).

In Leviticus 14:15-18 we read, "And the priest shall take of the log of oil, and pour it into the palm of his own left hand: and the priest shall dip his right finger in the oil that is in his left hand, and shall sprinkle of the oil with his finger seven times before the Lord: And of the rest of the oil that is in his hand shall the priest put upon the tip of the right ear of him that is to be cleansed, and upon the thumb of his right hand, and upon the great toe of his right foot, upon the blood of the trespass— offering: And the remnant of the oil that is in the priest's hand he shall pour upon the head of him that is to be cleansed: and the priest shall make an atonement for him before the Lord."

We have set forth here, in type, the truth that the blood and the oil cleanse from sin and consecrate unto the Lord. The oil on the ear of the leper signifies attentive obedience, listening to the Spirit at all times. The oil on the great toe is a type of a holy walk—we are admonished to have our feet shod with the preparation of the Gospel of peace (Eph. 6:15). The oil on the thumb of the right hand of the leper denotes service to God. Thus, the believer will be listening to what the Spirit has to say, walking where the Spirit bids him walk, and working as the Spirit leads him to stewardship.

THE SPIRIT AND THE WATER IN JOHN'S GOSPEL

The Gospel of John is the salvation Gospel. We find the key to this glorious book in John 20:30, 31: "And many other signs truly did Jesus in the presence His disciples, which are not written in this book: But these are written, *that ye might believe that Jesus is the Christ, the Son of God; and that believing ye might have 'life through His name."*

The Gospel of John three times refers to water as having to do with salvation and spiritual living. Jesus said to Nicodemus, "Except a man be born of water and of the Spirit, he cannot enter into the kindom of God" (John 3: 5). Certainly no spiritually minded teacher or preacher would suggest that water in the literal sense washes away sins. Water in the verse just quoted has a spiritual meaning—it represents the Word of God. We are born (begotten) of the water (the Word) and of the Spirit.

John the Baptist came upon the scene preaching repentance, crying out, "The King cometh!" and scores went out to him to be baptized of him in Jordan. John baptized in water unto repentance, but he said, "There is One who cometh after me who is preferred before me. He will baptize with the Holy Ghost and with fire."

John baptized in water, but he plainly declared that the Christ would baptize in the Spirit. What was the baptism of John? What did it suggest or symbolize? The baptism of John was symbolic of death and judgment. He baptized those who confessed their sins. He plunged them into Jordan's waters, representing the death and judgment they deserved as unbelievers.

On one occasion a group came to John desiring baptism, but he refused to baptize them. He said, "O generation of vipers, who hath warned you to flee from the wrath to come? Bring forth therefore fruits meet for repentance!" (Matt. 3:7-12). In other words, "Prove that you have repented and I will baptize you." The baptism of John signified death and judgment.

At the entrance of His public ministry, Jesus came to John to be baptized. We know the story well: "Then cometh Jesus from Galilee to Jordan unto John, to be baptized of him. But John forbad Him, saying, I have need to be baptized of thee, and comest thou to me? And Jesus answering said unto him, Suffer it to be so now: for thus it becometh us to fulfil all righteousness. Then he suffered Him. And Jesus, when He was baptized, went up straightway out of the water: and, lo the heavens were opened unto Him, and He saw the Spirit of God descending like a dove, and lighting upon Him: And lo a voice from heaven, saying, This is my beloved Son, in whom I am well pleased" (Matt. 3:13-17).

We know that Jesus Christ had no sin, He could not confess His sin personally, because in Him there *was NO sin.* But he represented the sins of the whole world: "Who His own self bare our sins in His own body on the tree, that we, being dead to sins, should live unto righteousness: by whose stripes ye were healed" (I Pet. 2:24).

Since Christ represented us who have sinned, He must in every minute detail satisfy the holiness of God, and it was imperative that He go beneath the waters of death and judgment. This He did — *symbolically* in Jordan, *literally* on Calvary.

In John 1:1 we read, "In the beginning was the Word, and the Word was with God, and the Word was God . . . And the Word was made flesh, and dwelt among us . . ." (John 1:1, 14 in part). We know that this refers to Jesus, God in flesh. Jesus was the Word wrapped up in flesh, He was the Word brought down to man. Therefore, when we receive Jesus we are *IN CHRIST.* The Spirit applies the Word, the hearing of the Word brings faith,

179

faith exercised in Jesus brings salvation (Eph. 2:8; Rom. 10:17).

Being born of water (the Word) and of the Spirit declares the believer to be one with Christ. When we are born of the Word and of the Spirit, we receive the fullness of redemption purchased in the death of the sinless substitute, the Lord Jesus Christ, and we become new creations: "Therefore if any man be in Christ, he is a new creature: old things are passed away; behold, all things are become new" (II Cor. 5:17).

In Genesis 1:1, 2 we read, "In the beginning God created the heaven and the earth. And the earth was without form, and void; and darkness was upon the face of the deep. And the SPIRIT OF GOD moved upon the face of the waters." God brought a new creation out of catastrophe, and the same happens when a sinner receives Jesus. Jesus is the water (the Word), the Spirit is the power that draws us to God and "borns" us into the family of God through the Word of God. We then become a new creation in Christ Jesus.

Water is mentioned again in the fourth chapter of John, when Jesus asked the Samaritan woman for a drink. The woman could not understand a Jew asking a Samaritan woman for water, since hatred of the Jew for the Samaritans was well known. Jesus said to this poor, fallen woman, "If thou knewest the gift of God, and who it is that saith to thee, Give me to drink; thou wouldest have asked of Him, and He would have given thee living water" (John 4:10). He then explained to her that the water HE would give was within the heart—*"a well of water springing up into everlasting life"* (John 4:14).

The Greek words here translated *"well"* and *"springing"* could have been translated " a *fountain* of water *leaping* up . . ." Acts 3:1-11 tells of the impotent man miraculously healed under the ministry of Peter and John, "and he *leaping up* stood, and walked, and entered with them into the temple, walking, and *leaping*, and praising God!" Acts 14:8-11 records the healing of a lame man at Lystra under Paul's ministry: "The same heard Paul speak: who stedfastly beholding him, and perceiving that he had faith to be healed, said with a loud voice, Stand upright on thy feet. And he *leaped and walked.*" (Acts 14:9, 10).

These men had within their bosoms a fountain of living water springing up, leaping up into everlasting life—new life. When the Holy Spirit completely possesses and controls the heart, there is peace and joy beyond compare— "joy unspeakable and full of glory." A person filled with the Spirit does not put on a "spiritual show," but rather, the rejoicing and the praise of God burst forth in naturalness—yea, supernaturalness—and the genuineness of such an experience is proved by wholehearted obedience and daily consecration.

In John 7:37-39 we read of *"rivers of water"*: "In the last day, that great day of the feast, Jesus stood and cried, saying, If any man thirst, let him come unto me, and drink. He that believeth on me, as the Scripture hath said, out of his belly shall flow rivers of living waters. (But this spake He of the Spirit, which they that believe on Him should receive: for the Holy Ghost was not yet given; because that Jesus was not yet glorified.)"

God fills us with the Spirit—not that we might shout or praise God to our *own* satisfaction and joy, but that we might be rivers of living water, pouring forth blessings to those with whom we come in contact. God fills US in order that through us He may benefit others. The same Greek word translated "rivers" here is translated "floods" in

181

Matthew 7:25 and 28, and as "flood" in Revelation 12: 15 and 16, thus signifying that the supply is not meagre, not just a little trickle or a few drops, but *an abundance* of living water. God joys in blessing abundantly. Everything with which He has to do is given in abundance, and He wants us to abundantly distribute what we receive.

Have you ever stopped for one moment and seriously considered what would happen if every fountain on earth should be dried up in a flash? Water is imperative to life, water is life-giving and cleansing in its use, satisfying to the thirsty person. Water is powerful, it floats the mighty battleship and turns the wheels of industry. There are many, many good things we could say about water. It is no wonder God uses water to symbolize our salvation and its results. We are BORN of the water, the new birth puts within us a FOUNTAIN of water, and that fountain grows into a RIVER of water. Since we have to do with water from the moment we are born until we die, we certainly know how necessary water is. It is imperative to be born of God *according to the WORD of God,* through the Spirit of God—not according to religion or man's dogma or doctrine.

Concerning the Church, Paul said, "Husbands, love your wives, *even as Christ also loved the Church, and gave Himself for it;* THAT HE MIGHT SANCTIFY AND CLEANSE IT WITH THE WASHING OF WATER BY THE WORD" (Eph. 5:25, 26).

Concerning the individual, John said, "Now ye are clean through the Word which I have spoken unto you" (John 15:3).

Water baptism does not save, nor does it *help* to save. The WORD is the power of God unto salvation to everyone that believeth (Rom. 1:16). The WORD is the incorruptible seed that brings the new birth (I Pet. 1:23). And when we hear His Word and believe on Him, believe in His birth, death, burial, and resurrection "according to the Scriptures," we are made ONE with Jesus in God: "For ye are dead, and your life is hid with Christ in God" (Col. 3:3).

THE "NUMBER ONE" NEED TODAY

I believe the primary need of churches around the world today is for Spirit-filled, Spirit-controlled preachers, teachers, evangelists *and laymen!* It is "not by might, nor by power, but by my Spirit, saith the Lord of hosts" (Zech. 4:6). As it was, so it is. We have too much man-made, man-organized "religion" today, and too little God-directed, Holy Spirit-empowered ministry. Before the day of Pentecost, Peter said, "I go a fishing," and the other disciples said, "We also go with Thee." But AFTER the day of Pentecost, Peter, "being filled with the Holy Ghost," preached a sermon the results of which added three thousand souls to the Church! (Read Acts 2:14 through Acts 4:31.) From Pentecost forward, Peter fished for the souls of men!

Before Pentecost, Peter was boastful. He said to Jesus, "Although all shall be offended, yet will not I . . . If I should die with thee, I will not deny thee in any wise" (Mark 14:29 and 31). But we know the sad story. He cursed and swore that he had never known the Lord! Before Pentecost, Peter was self-sufficient; but after Pentecost he was God-dependent: To the lame man he said, "Silver and gold have I none; but such as I have give I thee: *In the name of Jesus Christ of Nazareth,* rise up and walk!" (Acts 3:6).

Before Pentecost, Peter was doubtful. Seing Jesus walking on the water, he said, "Lord, IF it be thou, bid

183

me come unto thee on the water." But after Pentecost, *filled with the Spirit,* he thundered out, "THIS IS THAT WHICH WAS SPOKEN BY THE PROPHET JOEL; AND IT SHALL COME TO PASS . . ." (Acts 2:28).

Before Pentecost, Peter was impulsive and self-acting. In the Garden of Gethsemane, when the enemies of Jesus came with sticks and torches to arrest the Lamb of God, Peter drew his sword and cut off the ear of the servant of the high priest (Luke 22:50). But after Pentecost it was altogether different: "Be it known unto you all, and to all the people of Israel, that *by the name of Jesus Christ of Nazareth,* whom ye crucified, whom God raised from the dead, *even by Him doth this man stand here before you whole"* (Acts 4:10).

Before Pentecost, Peter was a coward, so frightened of a little maid that he denied his Lord in the presence of witnesses (Luke 22:56, 57). But after Pentecost he was courageous and bold: "Now when they saw the boldness of Peter and John, and perceived that they were unlearned and ignorant men, they marvelled; and they took knowledge of them, that they had been with Jesus!" (Acts 4:13).

Before Pentecost, Peter warmed himself by the devil's fire (Luke 22:55). But after Pentecost, he no longer needed to warm himself, because he had a fire within his bosom that warmed the inner man: "But Peter, standing up with the eleven, lifted up his voice, and said unto them, ye men of Judaea, and all ye that dwell at Jerusalem, be this known unto you, and hearken to my words!" (Acts 2:14).

This man Peter was certainly not the same after Pentecost. What was the difference? *The Holy Spirit made the difference!*

Consider Isaiah: He was a man of God; he was God's prophet. The crisis in his life came when he saw the Lord, "high and lifted up" (Isa. 6:1). He saw Jehovah in all of His holiness, and he cried out "Woe is me! for I am undone!"

The Hebrew word here translated *"undone"* means to be dumb or silent. In other places it is rendered "cut off" (Hos. 10:7); "brought to silence" (Isa. 15:1); "destroyed" (Hos. 4:6); "cut down" (Zeph. 1:11). Thus the testimony of Isaiah when he saw the holiness of Jehovah. The sight of God to the inner man of Isaiah revealed God in His holiness and made the prophet painfully conscious that he was not in fellowship and harmony with that holiness. He was "undone, cut off, brought to silence" when he beheld the holiness of God.

He cried out, "Woe is me!" He confessed, first of all, his own woefulness, and then he confessed the sins of his people: "Woe is me! for I am undone; because I am a man of unclean lips, and I dwell in the midst of *a people of unclean lips*: for mine eyes have seen the King, the Lord of hosts!" (Isa. 6:5). After his cleansing, Isaiah heard the voice of the Lord, saying, "Whom shall I send, and who will go for us?" And the prophet flung himself at the feet of Jehovah and in essence said, "Here am I! Send me! Crush me, break me, mould me and make me— SEND ME!" From that day forward, Isaiah was the powerful, spirit-possessed man that God could use.

Elijah is one of the most beloved prophets in the Old Testament. Elisha knew that Elijah was no ordinary prophet, and he clung to him, determined to get "the double portion":

"And it came to pass, when they were gone over, that Elijah said unto Elisha, Ask what I shall do for thee,

185

before I be taken away from thee. And Elisha said, I pray thee, *let a double portion of thy spirit be upon me . . .* And it came to pass, as they still went on, and talked, that, behold, there appeared a chariot of fire, and horses of fire, and parted them both asunder; and Elijah went up by a whirlwind into heaven" (II Kings 2:9-11 in part).

Elisha had followed Elijah from Gilgal to Bethel, from Bethel to Jericho, and from Jericho to Jordan. Then after Elijah was translated, Elisha took up his mantle, and others knew that the spirit of Elijah was resting upon him. They knew that Elisha now possessed the powerful demonstration of the Spirit that Elijah had possessed.

There are not many souls so rare as to have enjoyed a double portion of the Spirit's endowment. There are conditions to be met in order to receive that double portion enjoyed by Elijah. To receive a double portion, one must face the triumph of Calvary's hour over the life of Egypt. Egypt's sin must be ended: "And the Lord said unto Joshua, This day have I rolled away the reproach of Egypt from off you. Wherefore the name of the place is called Gilgal unto this day" (Josh. 5:9).

And then the Bethel of the living presense of the Lord Jesus must be recognized, moment by moment, day by day: "And Jacob rose up early in the morning, and took the stone that he had put for his pillows, and set it for a pillar, and poured oil upon the top of it. And he called the name of that place Bethel" (Gen. 28:18, 19). The Jericho of sin with its curse of worldliness and contamination must be forsaken, and finally, the Jordan of judgment—Jehovah God's sentence on self and self crucified with Christ—must be experienced. And when SELF is wholly done away with, crucified with Christ, then the

Spirit as the mantle of God's power, will rest upon the believer. Then the difficulties will give way before God's power, the bitter will become sweet, and we will be able to remove mountains, spiritually speaking, as we are led by the Spirit.

I do not intend to be sacrilegious or sarcastic in my closing remarks, but I must say that we are cursed with entirely too much spiritual ignorance in our churches today. I am not advertising my knowledge of the Word of God nor my wisdom through the power of God; I say with Paul, "I am what I am by the grace of God." But if ministers would forget their denominational convictions and personal beliefs and preach the pure, simple Word of God—line upon line and precept upon precept—instructing the people in "thus saith the Lord," instead of "Thus saith the *denomination*," there would be much less spiritual ignorance.

I doubt that there is any other subject in the Word of God about which there is so much ignorance today as that of the person and ministry of the Holy Spirit. He convicts us of sin, He draws us to Christ, He "borns" us into the family of God, He seals us until the day of redemption, He leads us in the paths of right living, and He will fill us completely if we will only allow Him to do so.

The Holy Spirit will not only give us the *"second blessing,"* but He will give us MANY blessings every day. There is no limit to the "rivers of living water" which the Holy Spirit can, and will, produce within us if we will only surrender completely to His power and influence.

The Believer and Suffering

THE BELIEVER AND SUFFERING

"Man that is born of a woman is of few days, and full of trouble. He cometh forth like a flower, and is cut down: he fleeth also as a shadow, and continueth not" (Job 1:1-2).

". . . For what is your life? It is even a vapour, that appeareth for a little time, and then vanisheth away" (James 4:14).

"For all flesh is as grass, and all the glory of man as the flower of grass. The grass withereth, and the flower thereof falleth away" (I Peter 1:24).

"For we know that the whole creation groaneth and travaileth in pain together until now. And not only they, but ourselves also, which have the firstfruits of the Spirit, even we ourselves groan within ourselves, waiting for the adoption, to wit, the redemption of our body" (Rom. 8:22-23).

"For we know that if our earthly house of this tabernacle were dissolved, we have a building of God, a house not made with hands, eternal in the heavens. For in this (tabernacle, or body) we groan, earnestly desiring to be clothed upon with our house which is from heaven: If so be that being clothed we shall not be found naked. For we that are in this tabernacle (body) do groan, being burdened: not for that we would be unclothed, but clothed upon, that mortality might be swallowed up of life" (II Cor. 5:1-4).

"The Lord is my shepherd; I shall not want. He maketh me to lie down in green pastures: He leadeth me beside the still waters. He restoreth my soul:. He leadeth me in the paths of righteousness for His name's sake. Yea, though I walk through the valley of the shadow of death, I will fear no evil: for thou are with me; thy rod and thy staff they comfort me.

Thou preparest a table before me in the presence of mine enemies: thou anointest my head with oil; my cup runneth over. **Surely goodness and mercy shall follow me all the days of my life: and I will dwell in the house of the Lord for ever"** (Psalm 23).

The last verse in the 23rd Psalm is David's way of saying: "We know that all things work together for good to them that love God, to them who are the called according to His purpose" (Romans 8:28).

David did not have the wonderful book of Romans, but he knew the truth of it in his heart when he said "Surely, goodness and mercy shall follow me every day I live — and then I will abide in the house of my Heavenly Father forever!"

In spite of what may happen to us as believers, we can be sure that **all things** work together for good to them who love God, who are called according to His purpose.

Because:

"What shall we then say to these things? If God be for us, who can be against us? He that spared not His own Son, but delivered Him up for us all, how shall He not with Him also freely give us all things? . . . Who shall separate us from the love of Christ? Shall tribulation, or distress, or persecution, or famine, or nakedness, or peril, or sword? As it is written, For thy sake we are killed all the day long; we are accounted as sheep for the slaughter. Nay, in all these things we are more than conquerors through Him that loved us. For I am persuaded, that neither death, nor life, nor angels, nor principalities, nor powers, nor things present, nor things to come, nor height, nor depth, nor any other creature, (tuberculosis, cancer, loss of friends, tragedy, or whatever troubles you) shall be able to separate us from the love of God, which is in Christ Jesus our Lord" (Rom. 8:31-39 in part).

Today as never before the question is asked, "Why do Christians suffer?" This question has been asked since Adam. Thousands upon thousands of godly people in all ages have asked, "Why did God permit this to happen to me? Why do I suffer?"

Thousands of believers have reasoned thus: "If God so loved the world that He gave His only begotten Son to suffer terrible agony on the cruel cross, why does He permit US who love JESUS to suffer sickness, heartache, persecution, trouble, pain, tribulation, grief, and (many times) tragedy? If God really loves us enough to do all the Bible tells us He has done for us, then why does He permit sickness, afflictions, and so much suffering? Why does He permit the demons of disease to continue to torment our bodies?"

These questions are not easy for a minister to answer, because in many cases — as in my own — ministers suffer, even to the very shadow of death itself. What is the answer to the question, **"Why do saints suffer?"** Some things are known only to God, but the Bible does give us some light on this perplexing problem.

In the many years I have been preaching the Gospel, traveling from coast to coast, from Canada to Mexico and into several foreign lands, I have seen some of God's dearest saints bedridden, disabled, sometimes suffering intense pain. I have looked into the faces of these dear saints and have seen the very love of God beaming forth from their eyes! At such times, I have asked "Why?" And then I remembered the greatest Sufferer of all who have ever suffered — the Lord Jesus Christ as He hung on the cross.

Some of you who will read these lines are sitting in wheelchairs. Some of you are lying in hospital beds. Perhaps you have searched your heart many, many times and have asked yourself, "What sin brought this suffering upon me?" Yet, after searching your heart honestly and sincerely, you confess that insofar as you know, all sin in your life is confessed and under the blood. When there is no known sin in your life, when your own heart does not condemn you and you know all is right between you and God, you may ask, "Why do I suffer? Why does God not heal me? I believe He is able, I know He CAN heal me, and I do not understand why He does not when I have prayed so fervently for healing."

Do not let anyone tell you that you are sick because of your sin, or that God will not heal you because you do not have the necessary faith. God pity preachers who are so heartless and cruel as to deal with suffering saints in such a manner!

To be sure, there are saints who suffer because of unconfessed sin; but that is not true in all cases. If you have searched your heart and confessed all your sin to God, you know your own heart better than does any preacher or evangelist.

THIS SCRIPTURE SHOULD BE READ BY EVERY BELIEVER

"Wherefore seeing we also are compassed about with so great a cloud of witnesses, let us lay aside every weight, and the sin which doth so easily beset us, and let us run with patience the race that is set before us, looking unto Jesus the author and finisher of our faith; who for the joy that was set before Him endured the cross, despising the shame, and is set down at the right hand of the throne of God.

"For consider Him that endured such contradiction of sinners against Himself, lest ye be wearied and faint in your minds. Ye have not yet resisted unto blood, striving against sin. And ye have forgotten the exhortation which speaketh unto you as unto children, My son, despise not thou the chastening of the Lord, nor faint when thou art rebuked of Him: FOR WHOM THE LORD LOVETH HE CHASTENETH, AND SCOURGETH EVERY SON WHOM HE RECEIVETH. If ye endure chastening, God dealeth with you as with sons; for

194

what son is he whom the father chasteneth not? But if ye be without chastisement, whereof all are partakers, then are ye bastards, and not sons. Furtherfore we have had fathers of our flesh which corrected us, and we gave them reverence: shall we not much rather be in subjection unto the Father of spirits, and live? For they verily for a few days chastened us after their own pleasure; **but He for our profit, that we might be partakers of His holiness.**

"Now no chastening for the present seemeth to be joyous, but grievous: nevertheless afterward it yieldeth the peacable fruit of righteousness unto them which are exercised thereby. Wherefore lift up the hands which hang down, and the feeble knees; and make straight paths for your feet, lest that which is lame be turned out of the way; but let it rather be healed. Follow peace with all men, and holiness, without which no man shall see the Lord: Looking diligently lest any man fail of the grace of God; lest any root of bitterness springing up trouble you, and thereby many be defiled" (Heb. 12:1-15).

This chapter is self-explanatory. We are to consider the great cloud of witnesses who have lived, died, and gone on to be with the Lord. We are to remember that all of these died in faith, many of them suffered. Hebrews 11 is the "roll call of the faithful." Read it carefully and you will find that many of God's dearest suffered horrible deaths in martyrdom; but we are not to look to these — we are to remember and consider them, but we are to look to Jesus **"the Author and Finisher of our faith."** Jesus set the example; He suffered **"unto blood"** to make it possible for us to be delivered from sin.

Verse 6 is very clear: "Whom the Lord loveth, He chasteneth, and **scourgeth every son whom he receiveth."** According to this verse, no child of God is excluded from chastisement. **All are included;** all children of God are chastened by the Lord. Verse seven is also very clear: If we endure chastening, God is dealing

195

with us as with sons, "for what son is he whom the father chasteneth not?" Any father who loves his children chastens and corrects them.

Verse 8 is dynamite: If we be without chastisement (whereof all are partakers) then we have not been born of the spirit and we are spiritual illegitimates. Every born again, blood-washed, redeemed child of God is chastened, and if we are not chastened we are not children of God! I beg you to see this, in spite of the high pressure preachers today who proclaim that God heals all and sundry who have the necessary faith. We become so accustomed to trusting in self and looking at things around us, many times God must lay us flat of our backs in a hospital bed to cause us to **look up.**

This is not true in all cases, not by any means; but many times it is the case. You may rest assured that God does chasten EVERY son — not one is excluded; and if we are not chastened we are NOT sons of God, we are sons of the devil and have never been born again. This is a clear Bible fact that all should see.

It will be a happy day in the lives of some believers when they recognize the fact that God gave up the body to return to dust. God made provision for the spirit in Genesis 3:15, but to Adam God declared, "Dust thou art, to dust thou shalt return." Some believers refuse to face the fact that these bodies are tabernacles of clay and are destined to suffer until Jesus comes in the first resurrection when we will be changed and will receive a glorified body. Our loved ones who have died in the Lord are resting with Jesus. They have some kind of spiritual body now, but they do not have their eternal, resurrection body. All believers who have died will receive that body when the Rapture occurs (I Thess. 4:13-18; I Cor. 15:51-55). All living believers will be changed in a moment, "in the twinkling of an eye," at the coming of Jesus, and all believers — living or dead — will receive a body like the glorified body of Jesus (I John 3:1-3).

There are many, many reasons why Christians suffer. The Word of God reveals that even the most holy of believers will be tested, tried — and will suffer until that grand and glorious morning when we see Him face to face in our glorified bodies.

There are lessons to be learned by believers that can be learned only in the school of suffering or in the university of pain. Jesus set the example: "It became Him, for whom are all things, and by whom are all things, in bringing many sons unto glory, to make the captain of their salvation perfect through sufferings" (Heb. 2:10).

"For in that He Himself hath suffered being tempted, He is able to succour them that are tempted" (Heb. 2:18).

Yes, the Lord Jesus took a body (Heb. 2:9) that in His body He could suffer as we suffer, and taste life in every respect in which we taste life, yet without sin. He never murmured or complained about His suffering. He suffered as no other human has ever suffered. Jesus was human, yet He was divine — He was God in flesh (II Cor. 5:19). Jesus set the example: He suffered, He was wounded — yet He opened not His mouth.

The Lord Jesus said, "In the world YE SHALL HAVE TRIBULATION: but be of good cheer; I have overcome the world" (John 16:33). My precious sufferer, rest assured that Jesus was where you are. But you may say, "Brother Greene, Jesus never went to the hospital. Jesus was never in a wheelchair." Jesus came to pay sin's debt and take the sinner's place; and just before He died He said to the Heavenly Father, "It is finished!" (John 19:30). He finished every detail of the demands of Almighty God. He tasted life, death, hell and the grave, and conquered all. Today He has the keys of hell and death (Rev. 1:18).

197

Weary pilgrim, cheer up! In the world you shall suffer persecution, tribulation, distress; but Jesus overcame. He walked every step you will ever walk; He suffered every pain you have ever suffered or ever will suffer; He suffered every anxious moment; He had a broken heart — **He knows!** Cast your care upon Him.

Speaking to born again believers on his first missionary journey, Paul "exhorted them to continue in the faith, and that we must through much tribulation enter into the kingdom of God (Acts 14:22). Do not forget, **"Whom the Lord loveth, He chasteneth."**

If you hear anyone make the statement that God loves us too much to permit us to suffer, mark it down that that person is spiritually ignorant and unlearned. Any minister who studies and rightly divides the word of truth will tell his people that **in this body we will suffer.** We will leave this world in pain if we depart this life before Jesus comes in the Rapture. We enter this world through agony and begin this life with a cry. We live in a body destined to hurt, to be sick, and to know pain until our race is run — and then we depart this life in pain, leaving our loved ones to suffer as we leave this life for another world.

When we are saved, that is the beginning of our salvation. When God saves us He begins a work which has for its final goal making us into the image of His Son, Jesus Christ. Until we are **conformed to that image,** He will not spare tribulation, pain, sorrow, suffering, testing — whatsoever is required to finish the task and make us like unto Himself. Our Lord and Saviour Jesus Christ was not exempt from suffering.

The truth of the whole matter is simply this: We do not suffer because God does not love us, nor in every instance because we have sinned. God permits us to suffer because He

DOES love us. He permits us to suffer in order that He may teach us the precious, priceless lessons and give to us the priceless blessings which can only come to us in the school of suffering.

The reasons believers suffer are legion. Sometimes, through suffering, God teaches patience. Sometimes, through suffering, God makes us strong. Sometimes He lets us suffer to test our faith, to prepare us for a greater ministry or for a harder test later in life. But whenever, however, or whatever we suffer, it is always **for the glory of our God.**

Christians know no such thing as "luck." Never refer to a believer as being "lucky." Believers are exceedingly blessed, and we profit exceedingly by the longsuffering of God. All things that transpire in the life of a Christian are for our good and for God's glory. There are no accidents with Christians. God does not **put** many things upon us, but He **permits** many things to come upon us for various and sundry reasons.

Mother, father, as you sit in the wheelchair or lie upon your hospital bed, be not dismayed or discouraged. The Master Potter is molding your life, making you into a thing of beauty to His honor and glory. You will never know the impact your smile and your beaming face can have upon those who come and go in your shut-in room. It may seem hard for you now, you may not understand it, but you may rest assured that if you are a good soldier and patiently wait for deliverance, you can claim the promise, "IF WE SUFFER WITH HIM, WE SHALL ALSO REIGN WITH HIM" (II Tim. 2:12). It is true that believers are not always punished through sickness for unconfessed sin, but let us look further into God's Word:

"But let a man examine himself, and so let him eat of that bread, and drink of that cup. For he that eateth and drinketh unworthily, eateth and drinketh damnation to himself, not discerning the Lord's body. For this cause many are weak and sickly among you, and many sleep. For if we would judge ourselves, we should not be judged. **But when we are judged, we are** chastened of the Lord, that we should not be condemned with the world" (I Cor. 11:28-32).

This one exception is clearly set forth in the Word of God. There is a sickness among born again believers for which there is no excuse; it is uncalled-for and should not be. There are many Christians who are sick and laid aside on the shelf who could be well, if they would confess their sins and walk uprightly. I am speaking of weakness and sickness pointed out in the passage we have just read. A person who is sick in such instances cannot be helped by hospitals, doctors, surgeons, nor drugs. Such sickness is the corrective, chastening hand of God's judgment. Speaking to born again believers in the church at Corinth, Paul warned them to examine themselves and not eat the bread nor drink the fruit of the vine at the Lord's table without first judging themselves. If they do, they are drinking damnation to themselves.

The Lord's supper is not to be taken lightly. When believers come together in the house of the Lord to remember the Lord's death in breaking of bread and drinking of the fruit of the vine, they partake the most solemn and important of the Church Ordinances today. When we partake of the Lord's supper, we look back to the cross, look forward to His second coming — and we are commanded to **look within**, to examine ourselves. When we look at His bleeding hands and feet and His thorn-pierced brow, we remember the tremendous price He paid for our redemption. We are redeemed by His blood (Col. 1:14; I Jno. 1:7). When we take the bread and the cup we look forward to that glorious appearing of the great God and our Saviour, Jesus Christ. We should at that time search our hearts and pray, "O, God, create within me a clean heart. . . Let the

200

words of my mouth and the meditations of my heart be acceptable in thy sight!" The Lord's supper is tremendously important to the Christian. "For as often as ye eat this bread, and drink this cup, YE DO SHEW THE LORD'S DEATH TILL HE COME" (I Cor. 11:26).

There are many, many reasons why I know the Bible is God's inspired Word; but in the account of I Corinthians 11:17-22 we have sure proof that this book was not written by man. Speaking to the believers at Corinth concerning their behaviour at the Lord's table, Paul rebukes them:

"Now in this that I declare unto you I praise you not, that ye come together not for the better, but for the worse. For first of all, when ye come together in the church, I hear that there be divisions among you; and I partly believe it. For there must be also heresies among you, that they which are approved may be made manifest among you. When ye come together therefore into one place, this is not to eat the Lord's supper. For in eating every one taketh before him his own supper: and one is hungry, and another is drunken. What? have ye not houses to eat and to drink in? or despise ye the church of God, and shame them that have not? What shall I say to you? Shall I praise you in this? I praise you not!" (I Cor. 11:17-22).

If a man who belonged to the Corinthian church had written I Corinthians, you may rest assured that he would not have revealed that some of the good members were behaving in a very disorderly manner in God's house around the Lord's table; but Paul rebukes them in no uncertain terms. He does not soft-pedal the message, but rebukes them sternly. He then warns that if they eat the bread and drink the cup unworthily they SHALL BE GUILTY OF THE BODY AND THE BLOOD OF THE LORD. He admonishes them, "Examine yourselves! Eat the bread and drink the cup in a worthy manner — not unworthily, for they that eat and drink unworthily eat and drink damnation to themselves." (The Greek word for damnation should read "judgment or destruction.")

Paul then goes on to explain that because they are divided, because they are practicing heresy and making gluttons of themselves, getting drunk in God's house, many of them are weak, many are sickly, "and many sleep" (they are dead) because they were acting ugly in God's house around the Lord's table. It cannot be denied that these words are written about believers. Thus, sickness, weakness, and death among these church members was the direct judgment from God upon them because of their sin.

In verse 31 Paul says, "For if we would judge ourselves, we should not be judged." Self-judgment is not an impossibility in the life of a believer. We can judge ourselves, watch our habits, and refuse to allow un-Christian things to come into our lives. Self-judgment avoids chastisement from Almighty God. But if we neglect self-judgment, the Lord must judge us through chastening. (But this does not mean condemnation.) Verse 32 clearly states, "But when we are judged, we are chastened of the Lord, THAT WE SHOULD NOT BE CONDEMNED WITH THE WORLD!" God lays the rod upon us to correct us, to steer us back into the straight and narrow way, to keep us from being condemned with the world.

That is God's holy Word. Believe it! It is altogether possible for a believer to be sick as a result of unconfessed sin. It is altogether possible that your sickness is the chastening hand of God, but it is not always true. Some of God's dearest, most consecrated children suffer all of their lives.

Paul clearly told the Corinthian believers why they were sickly, weak, and dying. They were misbehaving in God's house, they refused to judge themselves and repent. Many were weak and sickly, and many had stubbornly gone on in their self-will and lust until they were dead. Many believers in Corinth had died when they might be alive had they only repented of their sin and called on God for forgiveness.

When God saves a sinner, He does not give that sinner a license to continue in sin. "If any man sin, we have an Advocate with the Father, Jesus Christ the righteous: And He is the propitiation for our sins; and not for our's only, but also for the sins of the whole world" (I John 2:1-2). God wants His children to be clean and pure and holy. He will have His people clean if He is forced to lay the chastening rod upon them through sickness, sorrow and tragedy, the loss of health, wealth, employment or whatever. God will do everything in His loving, tender power to refine us and make us pure. And if we refuse to confess our sin and ask the Lord to forgive us, we then commit the sin unto death. John tells us if a brother sees a brother who has committed the sin unto death there is no need to pray for him.

If you are sitting in a wheelchair or lying on a hospital bed; if you are sick and shut in; and if with all your heart you have searched your own life and laid everything before God, confessing every sin of which you are aware, and still you are sick . . . you may rest assured your sickness is not from the chastening hand of God. Nor is it because of unconfessed sin in your life. God is permitting your sickness and suffering for another reason . . . a GOOD reason, because God Almighty never does anything without a good reason.

Personally, I believe most cases of illnesses among believers are not because of sin in their lives. I believe that only the minority of cases are because of unconfessed sin. A truly born again child of God does not enjoy harboring unconfessed sin in his or her life. We make mistakes — yes. We stumble and fall short of God's glory many times — yes. But we are sorry for our mistakes, we are grieved by our failures, and we long to go on our knees and ask forgiveness.

There is very definitely a **ministry of suffering**, just as surely as there is a ministry of giving, a ministry of song, of teaching, preaching, or evangelism. God calls and ordains people to witness for Him from a hospital bed and a wheelchair. Most times when I go to visit shut-ins to cheer them up, **they** cheer **me** up, and I come away feeling much better than when I went to visit them. So dear friend, if you are in a wheelchair, upon a hospital bed, in a sanatorium, please do not think that the worst thing possible has happened to you. Your suffering is a blessing in disguise, and there will be someone in heaven who would no doubt burn in hell had you not been called, commissioned and ordained of God to suffer for Jesus' sake!

It is not His power to work miracles that saves us. It is not His power to turn water into wine — but His power to lay down His life and take it again, that we might have life and have it abundantly. We are saved because of His sufferings — not because of His miracles, not because of His mighty works, not because of His powerful demonstrations in feeding the five thousand and walking on the water; but by His power to lay His life down and take it again (John 10:18).

"That if thou shalt confess with thy mouth the Lord Jesus, and shalt believe in thine heart that God hath raised Him from the dead, thou shalt be saved. For with the heart man believeth unto righteousness; and with the mouth confession is made unto salvation" (Romans 10:9-10.)

He was wounded because of our transgressions, He was bruised because of our iniquities. The chastisement of our peace was upon Him, and with His stripes we are healed . . . not His miracles, but **His stripes**. Jesus suffered as no one else ever has or ever will suffer. Through His sufferings, through His shed blood, through His death, burial, and resurrection, we have redemption. And in the sweet Bye-and-Bye we will have a glorified body that will never hurt, never be sick, and never die.

A THORN IN THE FLESH

"And lest I should be exalted above measure through the abundance of the revelations, there was given to me a thorn in the flesh, the messenger of Satan to buffet me, lest I should be exalted above measure. For this thing I besought the Lord thrice, that it might depart from me. And He said unto me, My grace is sufficient for thee: for my strength is made perfect in weakness. Most gladly therefore will I rather glory in my infirmities, that the power of Christ may rest upon me" (II Cor. 12:7-9).

In the first part of this chapter, Paul testified that he knew a man (I personally believe that man was Paul himself) who was caught up into the third heaven, the Paradise of God; and he saw and heard things there that are not lawful to tell. Surely that was a glorious experience! Many Bible scholars believe that this experience occurred when Paul was stoned and dragged outside the city of Lystra for dead; but believers prayed — and if Paul was dead God raised him from the dead, and he went back into the city.

No doubt Paul did see this indescribable vision. And because of that glorious experience, he says, "Lest I should be exalted above measure through the abundance of the revelations, there was given to me a thorn in the FLESH." Paul tells us that this thorn in the flesh was the messenger of Satan, to buffet him.

Paul did not complain; he simply relates for us a bit of his own intimate private life and experience with suffering, that we may be encouraged when we suffer. There are many reasons why God's children suffer sickness, bereavement, disappointment, heartaches. Paul did not suffer a thorn in the flesh because of sin in his life, he was not being buffeted by Satan's messenger because of something he had done. He was suffering to his good and to God's glory.

The glorious experience Paul had was fourteen years previous to the time he wrote about it, so we know that for fourteen years he had suffered this painful, grievous affliction. He had three times prayed to God in sincerity, perhaps with a broken heart and with eyes bathed in tears, that God would remove the thorn; but the Lord answered, "No: My grace is sufficient for thee! I have a reason for allowing Satan to buffet you. I would not have it any other way. I will not deliver you." I believe with all of my heart that Paul prayed in his heart, if not in audible words, "Thy will be done!" The Lord knew the heart of Paul; He knew Paul wanted God's best, and therefore He did what was best when He replied, "My grace is sufficient for thee!"

We do not know what Paul's thorn in the flesh was. The Word of God simply states that it was the messenger of Satan to buffet him. There has been much speculation concerning it, but no one knows what it was because the Bible does not tell us. But we do know that God permitted some affliction in Paul's life to keep him humble. Pride is one of the ugliest sins in the devil's catalog, and thousands of preachers and Christian workers today are cursed with pride. The Christ we represent was the most humble person ever to set foot on earth; and yet His representatives many times strut like peacocks! God forgive us — and keep us humble.

God has a way of making the devil's program backfire in his face. The devil probably thought he was hindering the ministry of Paul, that great spiritual giant who feared no one save God Almighty; but Satan had something to learn. The thorn in the flesh, "the messenger of Satan," did not hinder Paul. Instead, it proved to be a blessing in disguise. In II

Corinthians 12:9 he says, "Most gladly therefore will I rather glory in my infirmities, that the power of Christ may rest upon me!"

Aside from the Lord Jesus Christ I think there was never a greater preacher than Paul. To me, he was the greatest of the apostles. He had such an outstanding experience, and he was human — made of the same material as you and I. He was therefore subject to like passions. Had God not permitted the thorn in the flesh, it could be that instead of preaching Christ — crucified, buried, and risen again "according to the Scriptures" — Paul might have gone over the land giving his testimony!!!

Some of you dear people who read these lines will not fully agree with me, but it makes me spiritually nauseated when I read about some big time gangster, some alcoholic, some great movie star going all over the country drawing great crowds, with hundreds and thousands of dollars spent to advertise his appearance, magnifying his wickedness, giving his "great" testimony and experience! God Almighty passes out nothing BUT great experiences!! God does not give first-class and second-class experiences! Any conversion is great; any conversion is a miracle. Every born again believer has had a great conversion — never forget that.

Do you suppose, had not God permitted the thorn in Paul's flesh, that one day in Damascus there might have been a sign reading something like this: "You are invited to the city auditorium to hear Saul of Tarsus give his testimony"? We do not know what might have been the course of Paul's ministry had he not had the affliction to bear; but we do have this testimony in his own words: "Lest I should be exalted above measure, through the abundance of the revelations, there was given to me a thorn in the flesh, the messenger of Satan to buffet me, lest I should be exalted above measure."

Paul did not fully understand — that fact is clear, because he continued to pray for God to remove the thorn. God said "No" the first time, but Paul was not satisfied and prayed a second and third time. After three refusals from the Lord, Paul received an answer that comforted and satisfied him, and he did not pray a fourth time for God to remove the thorn from his flesh.

Paul's affliction brought him to his knees in humility, and while on his knees he learned grace he had never known: **"My grace is sufficient for thee!"** said the Lord. God assured Paul that with the thorn in his flesh he was much stronger than he would be without it. God said to Paul, **"My strength is made perfect in weakness."** That statement suggests that the "thorn in the flesh" was some physical illness that made him weak in his body but strong in the spirit. Strange as it seems, the thorn brought joy and gladness to Paul even though he suffered tremendously. He testified, "Therefore I take pleasure in infirmities, in reproaches, in necessities, in persecutions, in distresses for Christ's sake: for when I am weak, then am I strong." In and through it all, Paul learned submission, humility, surrender to God's will, a power he had never known, grace he had never experienced and joy that could never have been his had he not suffered the thorn in the flesh.

If we are to enjoy heaven's best and life abundant, we must learn the lesson "Not my will, but thine, be done!" Our will must be lost in God's will. It may be that God will put us on a bed of thorns in order to bring us to that place. Sometimes it is necessary for God to permit us to suffer in order to break our stubborn will. This is not always true, but it is true in many cases. Seemingly it was true with Paul, because Paul was a Jew, a free-born Roman citizen, one of the best educated men of his day. He sat at the feet of Gamaliel, the great teacher; he was a member of the Sanhedrin; he was a leader in the persecution against the church. The mob laid their coats at his feet when they stoned Stephen. Paul was no ordinary person. After his conversion he could have been exalted with pride and rendered useless in Christianity had God not permitted a thorn in his flesh. I am not saying that is true in your life, dear believer, as you sit in your wheelchair or lie upon your bed of affliction; I am saying it could be true. I do not know — but God knows.

I do know this: "If God be for us, who can be against us?" And we know that all things work together for good to them that love God, to them who are the called according to His purpose. If we suffer with Him we will reign with Him — and I can guarantee that Jesus will keep His promise. **His grace is sufficient for thee!**

When I was a little boy(I remember the incident as though it were yesterday) my father was about to give me good whipping. My dad did not use a belt — he used a peachtree sprout . . . a long switch. Just before he laid thirty stripes on my back, he looked at me with compassion and tenderness — and said, "Son, this hurts me much worse than it will hurt you!" I confess that I could not understand what he meant: but now since I have boys of my own and I have from time to time been forced to chasten them, I understand what my Dad meant. God is omnipotent, but He is concerned about every minute detail of our lives. It grieves God to be forced to lay the rod of chastening upon us, to put a thorn in our flesh; but God knows best and He makes no mistakes. So dear suffering believer, if you have prayed and sought deliverance, but God has not sent it, never forget that for YOU, suffering is more profitable to you and to God than perfect health would be!

God knows all the tomorrows — you and I know only this moment. God knows what will happen out yonder, while we only think we know. It will be a happy day in your life and mine when we can truthfully say with Paul, " . . . I have **learned** in whatsoever state I am, therewith to be content, I know both how to be abased, and I know how to abound; every where and in all things I am instructed both to be full and to be hungry, both to abound and to suffer need. I CAN DO ALL THINGS THROUGH CHRIST WHICH STRENGTH-ENETH ME" (Phil. 4:11-13).

WORDS OF WISDOM

"My son, despise not the chastening of the Lord; neither be weary of His correction: For whom the Lord loveth He correcteth; even as a father the son in whom he delighteth" (Prov. 3:11-12).

"He that spareth his rod hateth his son: but he that loveth him chasteneth him betimes"(Prov. 13:24).

"As many as I love, I rebuke, and chasten: be zealous therefore, and repent" (Rev. 3:19).

These words are out of place in most homes today, and in many pulpits. Today we are taught that punishing children is wrong, that we should not literally apply the rod, but that we should allow the child self-expression — a free hand in every natural desire. We are told that we should not interfere lest we give the child a "complex." I am speaking of the home and of our natural children, but when respect for parents is lost, respect for God and the church goes with it. When parents stop correcting their children in the home, the church stops Bible discipline and preaches the same Gospel spiritually that modern educators are preaching to our children in our secondary schools. **Self-expression leads to damnation.** I will guarantee that any child who is left alone to have free course to satisfy the desires of the flesh and of the natural mind, will end up in hell! The flesh has never been willing to obey and follow God, and never will be willing until God works a miracle in the heart. When God puts a new heart and a new spirit within

210

the individual, that is the miracle that makes the difference between a believer and an unbeliever.

Let me point out a Bible illustration of this: "In those days there was no king in Israel: **every man did that which was right in his own eyes**" (Judges 21:25). These are the last words in the book of Judges. The book of Ruth opens with these words: "Now it came to pass in the days **when the judges ruled,** that there was a famine in the land. And a certain man of Bethlehem-judah went to sojourn in the country of Moab, he, and his wife, and his two sons" (Ruth 1:1).

The last verse in Judges tells us that there was no king in Israel. Judges were in authority, and in that day EVERY MAN DID THAT WHICH WAS RIGHT IN HIS OWN EYES. The Book of Ruth announces that when the judges ruled, there was a famine in God's country, and a certain man left that country and went to the land of Moab. The name of that man was Elimelech and his wife was Naomi. They had two fine boys — Mahlon and Chilion. They moved from God's country into the land of the Moabites, who originated through the child born to Lot's daughter, and of whom Lot was the father (Gen. 19:33-38).

Elimelech and Naomi took their children and left the Holy land, to dwell in the land of fornication. Why? They were hungry. They could not trust God for bread and to take care of their physical needs, so they turned their backs on God's country and went to the land of lust and ungodliness.

They had not been there long when Elimelech died (Ruth 1:3), and the mother was left with two boys. (Remember, they had left God's country because of lack of bread — but now the bread earner is dead and buried!) The two sons grew up, and married daughters of the Moabites. Shortly thereafter, both of the sons died, and Noami was left with two daughters-in-law, having buried her husband and her two sons.

211

Finally, Naomi heard that the famine was ended in God's country, and she returned to the land of her fathers, the land of righteousness. When she entered the city of Bethlehem, the people said, "Is not this Naomi?" She answered, "Call me not Naomi, call me Mara: for the Almighty hath dealt very bitterly with me. I went out full, and the Lord hath brought me home again empty! Why then call ye me Naomi, seeing the Lord hath testified against me, and the Almighty hath afflicted me?" (Ruth 1:19-21).

During the reign of the judges, the people of God practiced self-expression; they sought neither God's face nor His will — they made their own plans. Naomi and her husband had willingly gone into the Land of God's enemies, the Moabites. Therefore God took the husband, permitted the two boys to marry women of the Moabites and then He took both of the boys. Thus Naomi was stripped of all that was near and dear to her heart. She returned home empty, broken, sad, and bitter because, said she, "THE LORD HATH TESTIFIED AGAINST ME, AND THE ALMIGHTY HATH AFFLICTED ME."

Naomi testified to the fact that God took her husband and her two boys, stripped her of all she held dear on earth — and finally she returned to Bethlehem where she belonged, where she should have stayed in the first place. Beloved, it would be better to starve to death in God's country than to be fat in the devil's country; but you may rest assured you will not starve if you trust God, because He will feed you. (He may not feed you everything you want, but He will feed you if you trust Him.)

What I am trying to point out is this: When we deliberately take our lives into our own hands and run them according to our own desires, leaving God out of our planning, then God whips us, chastens us, strips us, empties us — and brings us to

212

our knees. If we refuse to **come home,** God has a way **of bringing** us home — and He will do it!

There are many such instances in the Bible, but time and space will not permit me to discuss them in this message. May God help you to profit by Naomi's mistake, and whatever it costs you to give your best to Jesus, DO IT! Because if you fail to do so, God will certainly put the rod on you — perhaps not in the same way He chastened Naomi, but in whatever way best serves His purpose in your life. God loves every child He has, and "whom the Lord loveth, He chasteneth."

Peter tells us, "Beloved, think it not strange concerning the fiery trial which is to try you, as though some strange thing happened unto you: But rejoice, inasmuch as ye are partakers of Christ's sufferings; that, when His glory shall be revealed, ye may be glad also with exceeding joy" (I Peter 4:12-13).

It has been said that hard steel — the very best of steel — is **iron** plus **fire.** I lived on the farm, and I know good soil is rock that has been completely crushed and pulverized. Fine linen is flax plus the flail that pounds, the comb that separates and the shuttle that weaves. The most beautiful Chrisian life is brought about — not through paths strewn with rosebuds — but through affliction and suffering. I cannot explain it—but it is a fact no one can deny. If we are ever all that God wants us to be, we must be willing to have faith in Him and suffer without asking "Why?"

God's way is not our way, and suffering is God's way of doing things. I do not know why this is true, but God will give us the answer when we reach Home. His way is often through the storm, through the fire. His best is often found under the rod.

"He sat by the fire of seven-fold heat,
    As He watched by the precious ore.
And closer He bent with a searching gaze
    As He heated it more and more.

He knew He had ore that could stand the test
    And He wanted the finest gold,
To mold as a crown for the King to wear,
    Set with gems of price untold.

So He laid our gold in the burning fire,
    Though we fain would have said Him, 'Nay.'
And He watched the dross that we had not seen,
    As it melted and passed away.

And the gold grew brighter, and yet more bright
    And our eyes were so dim with tears,
As we saw the fire, not the Master's hand,
    And questioned with anxious fear.

Yet our gold shone out with a richer glow,
    As it mirrored a Form above
That bent o'er the fire, though unseen by us
    With a look of infinite love.

Can we think that it pleases His loving heart
    To cause a moment of pain?
Ah, no, but He saw through the present cross
    The bliss of eternal gain.

So He waited there with a watchful eye,
    With a love that is strong and sure,
And His gold did not suffer a bit more heat
    Than was needed to make it pure!"

"Whom the Lord loveth, he chasteneth; and scourgeth every son whom he receiveth."

In the years that I have been a Christian, had I not suffered, had I not been chastened of God, I would be afraid, and I would wonder if my experience were genuine or counterfeit. Chastening at the hands of the Lord is Bible evidence of His love; it is evidence that we are saved and are sons of God (Heb. 12:7). God does not chasten the devil's children; He only chastens His own; and if we be without chastisement we are illegitimate — we are not God's child. Chastening at the hand of the Lord is for our profit, for our eternal good, and even for our good while here on earth (Heb. 12:10). Such chastening brings forth the peaceable fruit of righteousness (Heb. 12:11). Chastening of God brings about holiness and holy living (Heb. 12:10), and makes the believer stronger in the faith. Therefore, a believer who is undergoing chastening, regardless of type or purpose, should rejoice instead of fretting, because chastening is definitely a blessing, not a curse. We shall never share the crown if we are not willing to suffer with Him.

It is true that "Now no chastening for the present seemeth to be joyous, but grievous: nevertheless afterward it yieldeth the peaceable fruit of righteousness unto them which are exercised thereby" (Heb. 12:11). Certainly we all confess it is not pleasant to go through trouble, sickness, heartache, tears and sorrow. It is not pleasant to be shut in when we would like to be out and about our business of witnessing, attending church, doing other things that we feel are so important and necessary; and yet — if we are willing to accept God's will for our life, we must face the fact that the Lord recognizes our condition. He sees our tears, He knows every anxious moment, and He permits these things to be. Since He holds all of our tomorrows in His hand, He knows best. What we need to do is pray for God to give us **grace to believe,** nothing doubting.

God gives us assurance that suffering will yield peaceable fruit — the fruit of righteousness and holiness . . . "UNTO THEM WHICH ARE EXERCISED THEREBY." This certainly teaches that if we are exercised by the trials, difficulties, sorrows, heartaches, pain, woe, and misery that come upon us, peaceable fruit is the result. But if we fret and rebel and grumble, the Lord may be forced to use even more drastic means to bring us to the place where He wants us. "Wherefore, lift up the hands which hang down, and the feeble knees; and make straight paths for your feet, lest that which is lame be turned out of the way; but let it rather be healed. Follow peace wih all men, and holiness, without which no man shall see the Lord" (Heb. 12:12-14).

Suffering saint, discouraged Christian, despondent believer, lift up your feeble hands. Turn your eyes upon Jesus, look full in His wonderful face.

And remember — If God be for us, who can be against us? For we know that "neither death, nor life, nor angels, nor principalities, nor powers, nor things present, nor things to come, nor height, nor depth, nor any other creature, shall be able to separate us from the love of God, which is in Christ Jesus our Lord." With such promises, look to Him and remember that He will not permit anything to happen to you that will not be for your good and for His glory. Understand it? . . . We are not supposed to! "The just shall live by faith" (Rom. 1:17).

BELIEVERS AND DIVINE HEALING

"Is any among you afflicted? Let him pray. Is any merry? Let him sing psalms. Is any sick among you? Let him call for the elders of the church; and let them pray over him, anointing him with oil in the name of the Lord: And the prayer of

216

faith shall save the sick, and the Lord shall raise him up; and if he have committed sins, they shall be forgiven him. Confess your faults one to another, that ye may be healed. The effectual fervent prayer of a righteous man availeth much" (James 5:13-16).

This is the age of much division and many opinions concerning divine healing and prayer for the sick. There are many interpretations concerning the matter. Some go off the deep end one way, and some go to the other extreme. Some declare that any person can be healed of any thing if they have the faith. There are others who teach that there is no divine healing at all in this day of grace.

We are not to dictate to God, but we are to request of Him the things we need according to His will. This passage in James has caused much discussion and division among Christian people. There are those who tell us that this Epistle does not apply to the church age at all. They say the opening words declare that it is not for anyone except Israel: "James, a servant of God and of the Lord Jesus Christ, to the twelve tribes which are scattered abroad, greeting" (Jas. 1:1).

This verse causes some to say that James wrote only to the Jews (the twelve tribes); but suppose he did write only to the twelve tribes? Does that mean that we cannot apply the teaching to believers in the church age? Certainly James wrote in the first century of the church age, and Paul declares, "All Scripture is given by inspiration of God, and is profitable for doctrine, for reproof, for correction, for instruction in righteousness" (II Tim. 3:16). I agree that Scripture has a primary interpretation and application; but we can learn lessons from Noah and the ark, from Lot and Sodom, and certainly those Scriptures were not directed to the church; but the things that happened were for our instruction and correction.

Even had James written to the "twelve tribes scattered abroad," the people to whom he wrote, if they were saved, were certainly members of the New Testament church. So I see no reason why anyone should outlaw the book of James for believers. We must remember that most of the Christians in the day of James were Jews. There were very few Gentiles who had been born again when James wrote the epistle that bears his name.

But the Word of God is self-explanatory, it carries its own light: "Is any sick among you? Let him call for the elders of the church." That settles it. Certainly James would not have invited the sick to send for the elders of the church if the message had nothing to do with the church age. The Scriptures do not say, "Call for the elders of the twelve tribes of Israel," but "Call for the elders of **the church!**" Certainly we have a perfect right to apply this teaching to the believers in the church.

There is a second interpretation of this passage. There are those who claim there is no supernatural miracle involved here, and that during the days when James lived and wrote the epistle, oil was a medicine, used many times in a medical sense. They point to the account of the good Samaritan where oil and wine were poured into the wounds of an injured man (Luke 10:30-37). They maintain that the elders simply prescribed the medicine for the disease of the sick person, and that the elders were doctors rather than religious healers or men of prayer. This group explains away the supernatural power of divine healing.

There is a third group who accept this Scripture as the New Testament teaching in this day concerning prayer for the sick. Personally, I agree with this interpretation. I am not fanatical on divine healing, but I know if there IS any healing, it is **divine.** God has worked miracles in my immediate family.

218

My son David is alive today because God touched his body. It is a long story, and I cannot go into detail here; but when David was three and one-half months old he was given up by the best of doctors and surgeons as a hopeless case. I asked my radio friends to pray for him. His older brother Tommy, very small at that time, went with Mrs. Greene and myself back into the woods, where we knelt by a big pine tree. I shall never forget the prayer little Tommy prayed for his baby brother. God heard our prayers, He touched David, and David is very much alive today, although the doctors said he would surely die in infancy. God made our bodies, and if it is His will, He can (and in many instances does) heal in a miraculous way.

Twice in my own life in recent years God reached into the very jaws of death and brought me out in answer to the prayers of His dear people. My wife is the one person whom I had rather have pray for me than any other person on this earth — I have more confidence in her prayers than in the prayers of any other person. The last time I almost departed this life I called my wife, then I called Tommy, David, and my sister. My wife anointed my forehead with olive oil, and she, together with the boys and my sister, bowed around me, and they prayed. Within the next hour I went into the hospital where I received nineteen pints of blood in transfusions. The radio audience prayed, and God raised me up. I thank God for my doctor, for the blood donors, for the technicians who gave the transfusions, for the hospital — for everything that was done for me. But I give God credit for healing my body.

James 5 is not for all classes of sickness, but rather for a limited group of suffering Christians who are sick for a very definite and specific reason. Healing is promised when sin is confessed and the prayer of faith is prayed. When we understand this and rightly divide the Word, we will have no difficulty with this passage.

The formula for healing as given here concerns believers who are sick because of willful, unconfessed sin in their lives. They could not be healed through medicine or surgery. The only healing for a believer who is sick because of unconfessed sin is repentance toward God, and faith for healing. Let me repeat, that does not mean that all sickness among believers is due to unconfessed sin; but as set forth in I Corinthians chapter 11, many were weak, some were sick, and some were dead because they had misbehaved at the Lord's table.

"But let a man examine himself, and so let him eat of that bread, and drink of that cup. For he that eateth and drinketh unworthily, eateth and drinketh damnation (judgment) to himself" (I Cor. 11-28-29).

God wants His children clean, spotless at all times, under all conditions. Holiness is the standard set by Almighty God and He is pleased with nothing less. God has made provision for cleansing, and if we will examine ourselves, repent and confess our sin, we will escape sickness and judgment sent upon us because of unconfessed sin. We have the promise, "If we confess our sins (this refers to believers) He is faithful and just to forgive us our sins and to cleanse us from all unrighteousness" (I John 1:9).

If you will read the opening verses of that chapter, you will see that the first Epistle of John is directed to believers, not to sinners. It was written and given to the church that we might enjoy **full joy** and life abundant — the spiritual birthright of every born again child of God. If a believer neglects God's cleansing through confession of sin, if he refuses to accept God's forgiveness by confessing His sin, then God must chasten that believer.

Paul told the Corinthians (and it certainly applies to us) that if we would judge ourselves, we should not be judged. But if we refuse to judge ourselves, then we are chastened of the Lord to bring us back and cause us to repent, lest we be condemned with th world. "For whom the Lord loveth He chasteneth, and scourgeth every son whom he receiveth" (Heb. 12:6). I am sure that James 5 is speaking of this group . . . those who are sick and afflicted because of unconfessed sin, because of a stubborn will that refuses to repent and return unto the Lord.

Suppose we look at the formula again: James said, "Is any sick among you? Let him call for the elders of the church." Please notice: James did not say, "Is any sick among you? **Let him be carried by his friends to the church to be prayed for there.**" If there are sick believers in the community, the elders of the church are supposed to go to the bedside of the person who is sick — the sick one does not go to the elders. There is not one word in the entire passage to suggest that the sick are to be carried to the church or to a meeting. They are to be prayed for in the home or wherever they are.

It is crystal clear that "the prayer of faith shall **save the sick,** and the Lord shall raise him up; and if he have committed sins, they shall be forgiven him" (James 5:15). It is the elders who pray the prayer of faith — not the sick one . . . Please notice, it does not say "the prayer of faith shall **heal the sick."** It says, "The prayer of faith shall SAVE the sick." Before there can be any healing in the life of the believer who is sick because of unconfessed sin, the sin must first be confessed to God, and upon confession of that sin the prayer prayed by the elders of the church will be heard by God and the sick one will be saved from death.

. . . . "If he have committed sins, they shall be forgiven him." The whole matter in James 5 has to do with unconfessed sins. James admonishes "Confess your faults one to another, and pray one for another, that ye may be healed. The effectual fervent prayer of a righteousness man availeth much." Confession of sin is the one requirement and condition demanded for healing and anointing the sick in James 5.

Humble confession by the one who has committed sin and is sick, the one who has sent for the elders of the church, is imperative for healing. I believe this Scripture in James 5 has to do with a limited number of believers who are sick because they have failed to follow the leadership of the spirit and have followed their own self-will and way, instead of yielding their bodies and their members to the Lord Jesus and the Leadership of the Holy Spirit.

I cannot overemphasize that it is not the faith of the sick that brings healing, but the prayer of faith prayed by the elders of the church. In our modern healing meetings, when the sick person is not healed, the healer informs the sick one that he does not have enough faith. If I understand James 5 correctly, it is not the sick one who does the praying, it is not the sick one who has the faith — it is the elders who pray the prayer of faith and the sick one is healed.

Job's sickness was not because of sin in His life; it was for the purpose of vindicating God's marvelous grace. Jesus said the sickness and death of Lazarus was for the glory of God (John 11:4), and Lazarus is not the only one who has been sick to the glory of God. We clearly saw that Paul's thorn in the flesh (some form of physical affliction) was for the purpose of keeping him humble. Paul prayed three times for God to remove the thorn — whatever it was — but God did not remove it. Instead, He said, "My grace is sufficient for thee!"

If we can suffer to God's glory, if we can bring forth more fruit through suffering and sickness, if we are yielded completely to God we will say, "Not my will, but thine be done." Remember God knows all the tomorrows — and He knows what is best for you and for me. We cannot apply James 5 to all cases

222

of sickness. This chapter has to do with a specific group and it is presumptuous for any preacher to read this Scripture in all cases under all circumstances, and pray expecting God to heal.

PAUL AND HEALING

"And God wrought special miracles by the hands of Paul: So that from his body were brought unto the sick handkerchiefs or aprons, and the diseases departed from them, and the evil spirits went out of them" (Acts 19:11-12).

Please notice in verse II, "GOD WROUGHT SPECIAL MIRACLES." God has a blueprint, a way of doing things, and we have no right to question God's way or God's motive. God is sovereign, and we have no right to question any act of His. The Apostle Paul was a special minister, a special vessel, a special servant, and God wrought special miracles at his hands. "From his body," (not from his office or his study) "were brought unto the sick handkerchiefs or aprons, and the diseases departed from them and the evil spirits went out of them." Paul had success in every case; no failures. Paul did not send word to some poor demented or paralytic person, "I am sorry — but you do not have enough faith. If you had the faith, you could be healed." Paul never sent such a message. Paul sent a piece of cloth from his body to the sick one, and the Scripture does not record that he ever lost a case! He was a special minister, a very special servant of God, and there has never been another Paul.

The miracles performed by Paul were for his day and time. There is no record in God's Holy Word that such healing was ever done before, or has ever been repeated. He had no failures. He sent the handkerchief or the apron, and the sick were healed. That had never happened before, and it has never happened since. The Holy Spirit is very careful to give us all the truth, the whole truth, and nothing but the truth. In this case God sent forth special manifestations through the Spirit, using Paul.

In Acts 28 we have an outstanding miracle at the hand of Paul. In Acts 27 we read of the storm and shipwreck as Paul traveled to Rome. He prayed to God for deliverance, and God delivered the men who were on the ship, although the ship was lost. In the beginning of chapter 28 they landed on the island of Melita.

The people on the island were barbarous, but kind. They built a fire, and Paul gathered sticks for the burning. As he laid the sticks on the fire "there came a viper out of the heat, and fastened on his hand." The barbarians saw the viper as it hung on Paul's hand, and they said among themselves, "No doubt this man is a murderer who escaped the storm and sea — yet vengeance suffereth him not to live." Paul shook the viper off into the fire, and the people expected to see him drop dead from the terrible poison of the viper. It was a deadly wound and the people on the island knew well that Paul was supposed to die; but when he did not die, "THEY CHANGED THEIR MINDS, AND SAID THAT HE WAS A GOD (Acts 28.6).

Publius, chief of the island, received the shipwrecked travelers, and lodged them for three days. The father of Publius was "sick of a fever and of a bloody flux." Paul prayed for this man, laid his hands on him, and he was healed.

Remember, beloved — this man was not a believer; he was a barbarian . . . a heathen. Paul prayed for him, laid his hands on him, and the man was healed. Do not forget that Paul was a "special servant of God." Of course, when the people saw the miracle, they brought all the sick, all the diseased — and Paul healed them all. When Paul and his party departed after many days, they were given many gifts.

The only reason I point out this passage is to show you that the Apostle Paul had a very special gift from Almighty God, and he used that gift to the glory of God on many occasions.

During the transition period — the first century of Christianity, many had special gifts and worked miracles that are beyond human imagination. But please notice this: Closing his second message to Timothy, Paul wrote: "Do thy diligence to come shortly unto me: For Demas hath forsaken me, having loved this present world, and is departed unto Thessalonica; Crescens to Galatia, Titus unto Dalmatia. ONLY LUKE IS WITH ME. (Luke was a medical doctor, a physician, Paul's last companion on this earth.) Take Mark, and bring him with thee: for he is profitable to me for the ministry. And Tychicus have I sent to Ephesus. The cloke that I left at Troas with Carpus, when thou comest, bring with thee, and the books, but especially the parchments. Alexander the coppersmith did me much evil: the Lord reward him according to his works: Of whom be thou aware also; for he hath greatly withstood our words. At my first answer no man stood with me, but all men forsook me I pray God that it may not be laid to their charge. NOTWITHSTANDING THE LORD STOOD WITH ME, AND STHRENGTHENED ME; THAT BY ME THE PREACHING MIGHT BE FULLY KNOWN, AND THAT ALL THE GENTILES MIGHT HEAR: AND I WAS DELIVERED OUT OF THE MOUTH OF THE LION. And the Lord shall deliver me from every evil work, and will preserve me unto His heavenly kingdom: to whom be glory for ever and ever. Amen. Salute Priscila and Aquila, and the household of Onesiphorus. Erastus abode at Corinth: BUT TROPHIMUS HAVE I LEFT AT MILETUM SICK." (Beloved, the great healer, the special Apostle, the man who sent handkerchiefs and aprons to the sick and they were healed, now leaves one of his best friends behind — SICK. WHY? I do not know. I only know Paul worked the special miracles that God wanted him to work, when God wanted him to do them, and then near the end of his ministry he lacked that special healing touch! Face it. It is Bible. God help us to face all Bible truth.) "Do thy diligence to come before winter. Eubulus greeteth thee, and Pudens, and Linus, and Claudia, and all the brethren. The Lord Jesus Christ be with thy spirit. Grace be with you. Amen" (II Tim. 4:9-22).

Paul, God's special minister, the man who wrought special miracles, was sick, downhearted, discouraged. Only Dr. Luke was with him; all others had forsaken and left him. Demas loved the world, others went hither and yon. And God's special servant, in prison, said "The time of my departure is at hand. Come quickly! Bring my coat — it is cold here. I left my good friend Trophimus at Miletum sick. Notwithstanding, THE LORD STOOD WITH ME AND STRENGTHENED ME." Paul is saying, "From the human standpoint the picture is dark; but the Lord is still with me." It was Paul who said, "Let your conversation be without covetousness; and be content with such things as ye have: for he hath said, I will never leave thee, nor forsake thee. So that we may boldly say, The Lord is my helper, and I will not fear what man shall do unto me" (Heb. 13:5-6).

Always bear in mind it was Paul who said, "And we know that all things work together for good to them that love God, to them who are the called according to His purpose . . . What shall we then say to these things? If God be for us, who shall be against us? Who shall separate us from the love of Christ? Shall tribulation, or distress, or persecution, or famine, or nakedness, or peril, or sword? As it is written, For thy sake we are killed all the day long; we are accounted as sheep for the slaughter. Nay, in all these things we are more than con- querors through Him that loved us" (Romans 8:28-37 in part).

I believe Paul suffered as no other human ever suffered, apart from Jesus Christ. He suffered more scars in His body for the sake of the Gospel than any person who has ever lived on the face of his earth, apart from Jesus Christ, and yet when he came to the end of the way he admonished a young preacher, "You preach the Word! Be instant in season and out of season! Reprove, rebuke, and exhort with all longsuffering. Do the work of an evangelist!" Paul gave this charge to young Timothy, his son in the ministry (II Timothy 4:11). What Paul said to Timothy is simply this: "I have preached the Gospel, I have suffered. It has cost me friends, fame, fortune. I have been whipped, shipwrecked, stoned and left for dead, chained in prison; but I have fought a good fight, I have finished my course, I have kept the faith. Henceforth there is laid up for me a crown of righteousness. Timothy, you fight the fight of faith. You preach the Word. If I had another life to live, I would preach exactly as I have preached, knowing what I know as I sit in this jail in Rome! Be a good soldier. Put on the whole armor of God — and suffer for Christ's sake, knowing that all things work together for good to them who love God, who are the called according to His purpose!"

If Paul left that message in his dying hour, if that was his admonition to a young minister, then I say, beloved, **God help us to be faithful** in health, in sickness, in wealth, in poverty, when people speak well of us, when we are criticized. God help us to do all that we do to His glory—without grumbling. If we are sick and shut in, God help us to know that HE knows best. Whatever God permits in our lives is for our good and for His glory.

I believe God can heal. I believe He can heal any disease that has ever been. I believe God can raise a person from the dead after they have breathed their last breath. But beloved, as ministers of the Gospel we must not dictate to God. We must pray the prayer of our Saviour: "Not my will, but thine be done."

I believe in praying for the sick, and I do pray for them. I go into homes and pray for the sick. I go into hospitals and pray for them, and many times after services I pray for the sick in the prayer room — individuals who come to me and ask for prayer. I believe in divine healing. (I do not believe in the practices of some who claim to be able to heal in this day; I believe there has always been the genuine and the counterfeit, and I believe this is true today.)

Do not ask me to name the counterfeit. I believe we have those who are counterfeit, but I refuse to call names. I judge nothing before the time. God will judge every man— and you may rest assured that when God judges, it will be righteous judgment. Therefore, I say I cannot condone some of the practices today, by men who claim to be healers. I believe in divine healing, and I believe there are some men on earth today who have faith to pray for the sick in a definite way. I pray for the sick, but I do not claim to have the faith to pray the prayer of faith. I know I have seen people healed in my ministry, but I certainly do not claim to possess the gift of healing. I pray the best I know how, with all the faith I have, but I do not claim any special anointing for any special gift of healing.

If there is any group of people on God's earth who have a warm spot in my heart, it is the sick, the suffering, and the handicapped. I pray for the sick daily, I pray daily for the suffering, and when I see a precious person who is handicapped my heart bleeds for that person. I would never abuse nor misuse a precious sick person or a handicapped person in any way. I pray for them, and I wish I could empty every hospital in the United States. I wish I could heal every handicapped person on earth — but I cannot. I pray for them, and will continue to pray for them; but dearly beloved, if you are suffering do

228

not blame Jesus. Remember — He permits suffering in your life for a reason, and He knows best. Never let the devil torment you by telling you that it is because of some sin. If you have confessed your sin, if you have laid your life bare before God and are still sick and shut in, cease to worry. Have faith in God and do not let the devil torment you about your sickness. Just remember that not all believers are sick because of sin. Some believers are sick to the glory of God, like Lazarus, Job, and others in the Bible.

In closing, let me assure each dear shut in, whether you are in a sanatorium, a wheelchair, or just confined to your home — if you are born again, if you are a true believer, you can cling to this promise: "The sufferings of the present time are not worthy to be compared with the glory which shall be revealed in us" (Rom. 8:18). Regardless of how much you may suffer, the God of Paul is saying to you, **"My grace is sufficient for thee!"**

We know even though we may not understand, that all things — the sweet and the bitter; laughter and tears; sickness and health; plenty and the bare necessities of life — work together for good . . . our good and God's glory. Therefore, in the tender words of Jesus to His disciples I close this message: "Have faith in God" (Mark 11:22).

DON'T CARRY THE BURDENS OF TOMORROW

God broke our years into hours and days,
That hour by hour, and day by day,
Just going on a little way,
    We might be able, all along,
      To keep quite strong.

Should all the weight of life be laid
Across our shoulders at just one place,
And the future, rife with woe and struggle,
Meet us face to face:
We could not go;
Our feet would stop, and so
God LAYS A LITTLE ON US EVERY DAY.

And never, I believe, in all life's way,
Will burdens bear so deep,
Or pathways lie so steep,
But we can go, if, by God's power,
We ONLY BEAR THE BURDEN OF THE HOUR.